RECLAIMING
THE
LOST SOUL
OF
YOUTH
MINISTRY

A Wesleyan Field Guide
Seedbed Publishing

RECLAIMING *THE* LOST SOUL *OF* YOUTH MINISTRY

BY JEREMY STEELE

 seedbed

Printed in the United States of America

Paperback ISBN: 978-1-62824-140-2
Mobi ISBN: 978-1-62824-141-9
ePub ISBN: 978-1-62824-142-6
uPDF ISBN: 978-1-62824-143-3

Library of Congress Control Number: 2014948244

Cover design by Brushfire Design Studio
Page design by PerfecType, Nashville

SEEDBED PUBLISHING
Franklin, Tennessee
seedbed.com
SOWING FOR A GREAT AWAKENING

To Laura
my amazing wife

CONTENTS

Part 3: Reclaiming Mission—Bigger Than Me

PREFACE

I have a hard time with faith. It's true. Belief is no big deal. If you want to know what I believe about an issue, I can talk your ear off—giving you a convincing argument for why I am right and why you should agree with me, but faith is a different issue altogether. Faith is putting your money where your mouth is and acting on your well-reasoned beliefs.

However, when we can find beliefs that are so deep and so true that they flow out in our actions in the world, *that* is where the power is. That is how movements begin and how lives are transformed, and that is where this book is trying to go.

This book began with an argument with a ministry colleague of mine in another denomination. We were talking about the kinds of things we do at our fun events and we couldn't have disagreed more with how they should be focused. We went back and forth arguing for a while, but it wasn't until I was in the car on the way home that I realized I had been thinking incorrectly about my ministry.

My friend and I were arguing over technique with success as our guide for whether or not something was a good or bad idea. The way we did our ministry had little to do with what we believed about God and much more to do with the techniques that the speakers at the big ministry conference told us were successful.

I had missed the point for over a decade. I had neglected to realize that what we believe about God should inform how we minister in his name. Or to put it in more technical terms, our theology should inform our praxis. That is what I had been preaching to my students for years: transforming belief into faith. Though I had been teaching it every chance I got, I had missed the application of this lesson in my own life as a minster.

That is when I began looking at the key tenants of my understanding about God and asking a simple question: If I believe this about God, what ministry actions does it require? I quickly realized that though I had several changes to make, part of the unique way I had been doing ministry was a result of my deeply held convictions about how God worked in the world.

The problem was that after much reflection I realized that there was another major source that needed to weigh in on my practice of ministry: church history. I have been fascinated for a long time with the movement begun by John Wesley and have admired much about his life and the innovations that he made in ministry in his time. I have sought to follow his example—both in living out the values he offered to the world, as well as trying to continue his spirit of innovation in my own areas of authority.

After almost another decade of wrestling with all of these ideas, I am writing this book as another voice in the conversation with the hope that, whether or not you share my particular theological or historical perspective, you will be challenged to work out what you believe and how it informs your work in ministry both personally and programmatically.

You will notice that each chapter starts with a story from my life about a moment of particularly unhealthy ministry that either my friends or myself had to weather in a less-than-perfect world. I offer these sometimes tragic, sometimes humorous stories as a doorway into the theological or historical task, as well as a way to keep our minds on the very practical issues that come about when considering the theme at hand in each chapter. From there, we will reflect on the particular theological or historical element and how it is given fullness through the insight of the Scripture. After all of that, we will explore how it impacts what we do as people who lead and/or plan ministry and how it impacts us personally as believers and leaders.

I hope this book will take you on the journey I have been on for the last several years. That it will cause you to consider how what you believe informs how you live and practice ministry. I hope that you will gather some of your fellow leaders and wrestle with this book together. I pray that the Holy Spirit will use these words to shine light on the path that helps you travel the distance between belief and faith.

ACKNOWLEDGMENTS

More than any other person, I am deeply indebted to my youth minister, Steve Beck, who modeled for me from the very beginning that youth ministry is more than scavenger hunts and cool fonts for lyrics on the overhead. I cannot overstate how his mentoring and soul-focused approach to ministry underpins every word in this book.

It is rare that you find a publisher as deeply committed to a work as the team at Seedbed Publishing has been to this unique mix of theology, storytelling, and practical ministry advice. I am indebted to J. D. Walt and Andrew Miller for their excitement as well as their unique ability to help focus this writer's vision into the most clear, compelling version of what I saw in my mind's eye.

A special thanks must be given to the people of Christ United Methodist Church in Mobile, Alabama, and to my brilliant Next Generation Ministry team who have helped me refine this book in our context and are charting an exciting course for engaging Wesleyan ministry to children, youth, and young adults.

RECLAIMING
THE
LOST SOUL
OF
YOUTH
MINISTRY

"J-Dub"—
An Introduction

(Why Wesley Matters for Youth Ministry)

I just want my life to matter," Jenny pleaded as she sat staring at me and feeling apathetic in the chair in my office. "I mean, I come to church and it's whatever, and I go home and, you know, we watch TV and I realized that if I died right here in your office my life would not have mattered at all." She looked away. "The world would be exactly the same."

That is the drumbeat of teen hearts all over the world. They see what's wrong with the world, they want to do something about it, but are paralyzed. With all they are, they want to change the world, but they don't know how. They don't know where to start.

Teens know that the judgmentalism of many of the Christians around them is far from correct. They know this because as these students grow up and watch their friends make bad choices, they still love them and want to be friends with them. When pressed many will confess their belief that unconditional love has the power to change people.

This, of course, brings me to "J-Dub"—John Wesley. Yes, he is the founder of Methodism and the author of a commentary on the New Testament. Yes, he is the guy who opposed slavery and helped all of the abandoned Anglicans receive communion during the split between England and the Colonies. But let's not be blind. He wasn't perfect. He had doubts and struggles and worked hard at following Jesus. All of this—his life and writings and ideas and the movement he helmed—are the key to successful youth ministry.

How does this dead white guy from the 1700s have any impact on successful youth ministry in the 2000s? It's simple: his life and theology work for today's students. He had this idea, this passion, that he might change the world. Not just convince it of a new idea about God or teach it as logical proof for God's existence, but that the world would be completely transformed from the inside out. He pushed with every second of his life to spark this change and see it spread across the globe.

But the true power for today's teens, the really amazing thing, is that he believed it was the overwhelming capacity of God's love that changes the world. Not a set of doctrines or an itemized answer to everyone's questions, but love. Wesley cast a vision of the world that was unlike anything before or since. It was a world where God actually cared about *everyone*, not just the chosen few who believed the right thing. It was a world where God loved us in the best way possible, unconditionally and un-statically. In other words, God loves us so much that he wants to use that overwhelming love to transform us into something better than we are.

Wesley's vision of the world was one where religion was not just about personal enlightenment and self-realization. For this brilliant innovator, God's love reached beyond the individual and focused on transforming the world as well. That meant that poverty was a spiritual issue as was health and education and injustice. Nothing escapes the scope of this boundless, ever-advancing love of God.

Thus, Wesley sat in a room and wrote a bunch of books about it, right? No. He got up and moved to the worst parts of town. He preached to the dregs of society *and* the high society. He lived out the love of God in the most difficult environments imaginable. And when this movement of God grew, Wesley delegated and trained leaders and rode thousands of miles on horseback helping individuals in cities all over the country.

And then he got filthy rich and retired in a big house, right? No! He was all in. Every bit of time and energy and money was spent on fueling this movement of the love of God as it rolled across towns and cities. Wesley gave freely and called others to do likewise. He didn't amass any wealth to speak of except that which resided in heaven as he poured every resource he had into changing the world.

I don't know about you, but that seems to be just about *exactly* what every youth I know wants for their life and their world. That is the kind of faith worth getting up early on a weekend for, and that is what we need to be offering.

Does that mean no more lock-ins and pizza parties? Would our celebri-pastor J-Dub want us to go around thinking deep things and having intense discussions only? Absolutely not, but it does mean that absolutely everything we do is touched by this pattern of life and theology. Every game, every sermon, every bus breakdown is imbued with meaning, and that is why we are here.

We are here because if we don't take a second and think about it, we might just take the ministry idea of any random person and do it ourselves, never realizing that it is part of the problem. When students hear what we just said and then experience the opposite, what we said doesn't matter.

Now is the time. It is time for us to reclaim a brilliant vision of life and ministry. It is time for us to live like we believe it, and it is time, most of all, to be agents of God's overwhelming love seeking to change the world.

Part One

Reclaiming Grace—
An Ordered Mess

*"It is the work of God alone to justify,
to sanctify, and to glorify; which three
comprehend the whole of salvation."*

—John Wesley
"Predestination Calmly Considered"

1

Wooing Lock-Ins

(Prevenient Grace in Pizza)

After a full day of rain, the air on the screen porch at summer camp where I was worshipping with a couple hundred students was thick. The close to 100 percent humidity combined with the ninety-plus degree heat was far from our minds. The place was silent except for the occasional scrape of a metal folding chair on concrete because we were all glued to the words of Brother Hale.

The evening before, he had caught our attention with part one of the end times and tribulation, and now he was unveiling the horror of the rapture to our adolescent minds. He was incredible. Without the aid of the yet-to-be-released *Left Behind* books or movies, Brother Hale talked about crashing planes, derailing trains, and failing power grids.

He had made it clear to us how thoroughly sin separated us from God. Nothing we could do could mend the divide, and we were living in a situation where we were hopeless and could neither hear the voice of God nor feel his presence. God wanted to bless us, but our sin prevented his blessings from flowing in our life. The altar was full, and I was saved.

I couldn't imagine how he could top that, but he was doing it. Now this Southern minister was about to take it to the next level and forever scar many of the kids sitting there. He was finishing his bit on the horrors of what would happen to those who had been left behind in the rapture—water turning to blood, boils, and every other atrocity Revelation made available to him—when, unbeknownst to us, a person carrying a giant horn snuck around behind the backs of the crowd on the other side of the screen waiting for the appointed time.

With the deftness of a carnival pitchman, Brother Hale raised his volume and sped up as he said, "You know what it says, in the twinkling of an eye like a thief in the ni—"

Before he finished the word, the horn blew, the lights went out, and the room fell silent for what seemed like an eternity until it was broken with the tears of the teens that had been left behind. Needless to say, I got saved twice more on that night . . . just to make sure.

• • •

Un-Graceful Preaching

There are layers of trauma in this story, not the least of which is the theological trauma created by the portrayal of a God who is only nice to the in-crowd and only cares about getting more people into that crowd.

To be honest, the matter of God's grace can be a touchy subject among those who like to spend their time arguing about theological nuances. For some, the grace of

God is only extended to us in order to forgive our sin. We experience it in fullness at that moment and it does its job once and for all. For others, there are moments where we experience it in lesser strengths at other times, but the fullness only at the moment of salvation.

For those who, like Brother Hale, relegate God's grace to the moment of salvation, that moment soars to the pinnacle of importance. I have seen more than one pastor with this understanding of the grace of God become obsessed with finding techniques for getting people to that point. They have diagrams and arguments. They develop tracts and evangelism methods that focus on getting people to "cross the line of faith." While this perspective is beautiful in its own right, and while I agree with a whole lot of its understanding of salvation, its limitations to God's grace come up short for me.

The Trinity of Grace

For those who follow the way of faith pioneered by John Wesley, we understand God's grace in much the same way as we do the Trinity. For us, we are constantly experiencing the fullness of God's grace in one of three forms. We will be spending the first three chapters talking about these forms and the brilliant ways Wesley made them clear. This chapter deals with my favorite: prevenient grace.

As we will discover, this grace is experienced by everyone everywhere. It is one of the pieces to explaining how many people who are not believers do not feel particularly separate from God. Rather, throughout their lives there are times when they are acutely aware of God's presence and blessing. Ask anyone who has children and they will tell you that as wild and somewhat terrifying as it is, you cannot deny the sense of intense blessing the first time you hear them cry and or the moment they grab hold of your finger with their tiny hands. It's a blessing that strikes awe in the heart of even the harshest skeptic. If God's grace and blessing only rest on Christians, we have a problem because there is no statistical difference between Christians and non-Christians in terms of fertility. They are equally blessed with children. Why is that? How could such a miraculous moment be so commonplace regardless of your devotion to God?

It turns out that God doesn't hold back on people just because they are not following him. We believe that all human beings, whether they are following Jesus or not, are experiencing and being offered the fullness of God's grace. They don't have to earn it or ask for it; they get it for free. This helps explain why some people have wonderful, beautiful, fulfilling lives despite never deciding to follow Jesus. Prevenient grace is the form of God's grace that is extended to all of mankind, and is the way that God chooses to express his love to those who do not know him in an effort to woo them to turn their lives to follow him.

Glimpses of Prevenient Grace in the Scripture

This idea is seen throughout the Scripture, but arguably nowhere more clear than in the words of Jesus in Matthew 5:45: "He causes his sun to rise on the evil and the good, and sends rain on the righteous and the unrighteous."

The sun and rain here are both very positive things in the more agrarian culture of the first century, and this talks about God using his resources ("his sun . . .") to bless everyone regardless of their nationality or religious preference.

In Romans 1:20, Paul talks about God's natural revelation given to all mankind. He says, "For since the creation of the world God's invisible qualities—his eternal power and divine nature—have been clearly seen, being understood from what has been made, so that people are without excuse." He reveals himself through sunsets, flowers, fertile soil, and the ability of the human heart to love.

Those are the external things, but prevenient grace goes far deeper, infecting the deepest parts of existence with God's grace. Philippians 2:13 acknowledges the grace of God within us saying, "It is God who works in you to will and to act in order to fulfill his good purpose." God's prevenient grace is also acting within us, imbuing all creation with a desire to seek to connect with God and do his will in the world.

In other words, this prevenient form of God's grace is what is responsible for drawing us to God. John Wesley expressed it by saying that prevenient grace is "the first wish to please God, the first dawn of light concerning His will, and the first slight transient conviction of having sinned against Him."[1]

A Prevenient Moment

Several years ago during the summer, our youth ministry kids and staff had grown close to a Nigerian minister while we were attending a mission camp. Not only were we all amazed at the strength of a faith that withstood being abducted by a Muslim militia, they were excited by his ministry. He was teaching classes to Muslims and Christians on how to use slow sand filtration to provide clean water and fuel-efficient cookstoves to eliminate smoke from the kitchens (the number-four killer in this area). He formed relationships through this demonstration of love that God was using to change lives and call people to follow Jesus.

Over the next several months students did little things here and there to raise some money to help send people to these classes in Nigeria, but there was a feeling that we needed to do something bigger. At the same time we were planning our yearly Super Bowl party (because God loves football too, right?). Like two linemen hitting each other in the opening play of the biggest game of the year, these two ideas collided, fueled by our passion for mission. "One Night for Nigeria" was born.

The event would still be filled with fun and games. There would still be the junk food and football on big screens, but now it had a bigger purpose. We got everything from the food to the inflatables donated by local businesses, and would take all the registration money that would normally cover those expenses and give it to our friend in Nigeria.

Now the youth ministry's obligatory "bring your friend" was bigger. We weren't just trying to get more people there—each person that attended meant more lives that would be saved across the world. The students not only experienced the fun, free-blessing love of God, but saw that this body of Christ was global. They saw that the image of God connecting us also meant trying to save Muslim children from dying by smoke inhalation in Nigeria. This was prevenient grace at its best, and much more.

Prevenient Ministry

As you can tell, I believe that this is the key to taking those fun events to the next level. This is the key to taking events that generally have students eating too much candy, playing ridiculous games, and often have you staying up way past your bedtime, and transforming them into an opportunity for spiritual transformation.

The church bills these ministries under the heading "fellowship" (which Doug Fields pointed out two decades ago represents a lack of understanding of biblical fellowship). They are fun (especially if you are the extroverted type), but what is the point? Why do them? Kids can generally have just as much fun at a sleepover at their own house, right?

Contrary to some of my more serious theological colleagues, I think these ministries are incredible assets to the kingdom. I think they have the potential to communicate God's grace in unique ways, and are ripe for being transformed into opportunities for prevenient grace as long as we seek to make them grace-driven rather than fun-driven. We need to focus on their purpose.

The purpose of a lock-in? I thought we just stuck them all in a gym and gritted our teeth until morning! That may be the case if you are the YMCA, but the church has a bigger purpose. These ministries often end up reaching out to the friends of your students and can end up with a large number of students who do not normally darken the doors of a church. When that is the case, the belief in the prevenient grace of God should impact our choices in those events so that they are geared to communicating that form of God's grace to the students in that event.

Don't worry, this doesn't mean that your lock-in has to turn into a fifteen-hour-long Bible drill. It means that instead of your purpose and focus being fun, it is on communicating the grace of God.

Focusing any ministry is powerful in that it helps give you new ideas while giving you parameters to delete others. If you look at the Scriptures we referenced above, you can pull out some simple categories of program elements that would be in line with a prevenient-grace ministry:

- Universal Blessing: Students who do and do not go to church should experience a positive feeling and/or a blessing.
- General Revelation: Students are allowed to experience, engage with, or share their experience of something spiritual without a requirement or expectation of any formal knowledge of God or instruction in faith.
- Imago Dei: Students are given the opportunity to discover within themselves aspects of spirituality or God.

Let's get real practical: Take a gross game where a student is going to get to cover themselves in chocolate syrup and slide down the center aisle of the sanctuary into the Baptist church's baptistery you borrowed. The fun of this game can communicate the universal blessing of God: Christians and non-Christians having fun together. Success! To take it to the next level you might try and incorporate some of the Imago Dei category by encouraging them to grab a friend the second time down the aisle and experience God's desire to be in relationship that is written into our human nature.

These same categories can cut in the other direction, helping to give the boundaries we talked about earlier.

- Universal Blessing: You do not do elements that focus on negative feelings of shame or embarrassment.
- General Revelation: You do not do elements that require some prior knowledge of God or the Bible (Bible drills, etc.).
- Imago Dei: You do not do elements that require students to utilize the ungodly attributes within themselves (Yo' mamma joke contest).

Prevenient Ministers

Prevenient grace has as much to say about who you are as a pastor as it does about your upcoming lock-in. If God is constantly extending his grace to those who are not even following him, the definition of who is in our "flock" becomes quite different. You are the pastor to everyone involved in your church's social network, and as a pastor (really, as a Christian in general), you are to be an agent of God's prevenient grace in all of those lives. You are to be the person who helps illuminate God's desire to fulfill their needs.

Everyone needs someone who is willing to hear their stories of pain and mistakes and offer God's loving words of forgiveness. Everyone needs someone who is willing to teach them about spiritual things and challenge them to a life focused beyond the here and now. If you are like most pastors, a vast majority of your time is spent on the people who regularly attend your church. What we end up doing in this case is causing the rain to fall on the churchgoers and not on those who do not attend. But the reality is that everyone needs a pastor.

Pastors who are trying to live into this role of being an agent of God's prevenient grace do things differently. They show up at a school that no one attends from their church and spend an hour or two serving the staff by volunteering in the office or making a Starbucks run. They spend some time at the local youth hangout spot having conversations about faith, listening, and offering forgiveness without trying to sell their upcoming event.

The influence of this belief stretches into every aspect right down to the conversation level. Prevenient grace changes our conversations. We no longer are introducing people to Jesus. We are no longer delivering to them something with which they have never been in contact. Instead, we are talking about the being who has been blessing, protecting, and wooing them for their entire life. We say things like, "I bet you know more about God than most people think" and "I know that you have had experiences with God before even if you didn't know it at the time."

This influence even challenges how we see the rest of the world. It helps us realize that we are all image-bearers of God. Everyone is a person of sacred worth whom God created as good to be part of making earth look more like heaven. If we can see through these prevenient eyes, we notice the pieces of others that echo their creator rather than the parts that have gone off track. We try our best to hold up a mirror that shows them the image of God that has been within them all along.

➡️ **Personal Processing**

1. Think of a recent conversation with a student who does not attend your church. How did you focus on the aspects of prevenient grace we described?

2. Make a list of five places you could go without being a creeper and make connections with students who do not attend your church.

3. What would you have to do to make your visit to those five places about prevenient grace rather than just about inviting the students to your church?

4. At what point would inviting them to your church be part of conveying prevenient grace? How would you do it without seeming like that was your only reason for coming/talking/ministering?

5. Look at your schedule. Carve out an hour in the next month (preferably next week) to do this type of ministry.

➡ **Ministry/Team Processing:**

1. Make a list of all your ministries that have a significant percentage of students present who are not involved with your church.

2. Of those, which are (or should be) focused on conveying prevenient grace?

3. Take each ministry and list each major piece.

4. Now it's evaluation time. Look at each piece and ask: Does this do a good job of conveying prevenient grace? Does it encourage actions or emotions that are contrary to those which prevenient grace implies? How can it be improved or with what can it be replaced?

5. Take a moment to discuss with your team how the personal processing challenged you. What is one thing you want to change or do differently as a result?

2

Cleansing Camps

(Justifying Grace through Ziplines)

But are you *sure* that you're saved? Do you know beyond a shadow of a doubt that when you die you will be in heaven? If not, it's time to cross that line today. If you're not sure, it's time to come down to the altar of forgiveness."

I went down. Sure, I had been baptized and confirmed and even prayed with someone at camp, but I wasn't sure. In fact, I had no idea how to be sure, but I knew one thing: I didn't want to go to hell.

I was at my friend's church for one of those pizza parties the night after the special speaker came to talk to our public school about everything *but* religion. We had screamed our conversations over Christian rap music and pepperoni, listened to testimonies, and the evangelist who had hidden his true profession at our school was delivering extra helpings of guilt and doubt as almost everyone went to the altar.

They ushered us out into smaller groups with tract-equipped volunteers, but there were so many of us that we spilled out of the Sunday school rooms originally reserved into every nook and cranny of the youth area. I ended up in the hallway in between the classrooms and the fellowship hall and was now face-to-face with someone I had never met. I tried to explain that I had made decisions before, but I had no idea how to *know* that I know that I was saved.

His response was simple, "Have you ever prayed the sinner's prayer?"

This was a totally new revelation! The sinner's prayer!? This sounded like exactly what I needed! How had no one told me about this before!? "No, what's that?"

"That's the answer you've been looking for. It's how you know that you're saved. All you have to do is believe you're a sinner, and say this prayer, and you are going to heaven! And the angels throw a party because you chose God!"

Somehow, this seemed too good to be true. The idea that my eternal destiny was tied up in three or four sentences seemed like a let-down considering the horrible depiction of hell and the almost unbelievable explanation of heaven we had just heard, but this guy seemed to know what he was talking about. I was in.

I prayed the prayer, and I *knew* that I knew that I was saved—at least for a while.

• • •

Preaching Doubt and Cheap Faith

I'm not even sure where to start with this story. Should it be the fact that this "evangelist" specialized in making Christians doubt their faith, or maybe that he took the immensity of the sacrifice of Jesus and boiled it down to a teenager choosing to read three sentences? How about the fact that there was a total lack of talk of the here and now and the decision was based exclusively on an eternal destiny that no one can comprehend or talk about from firsthand experience?

As difficult as it is to admit, this is nothing new. What was happening at my friend's church was similar to the temptation that Jesus faced in the wilderness in Luke 4. As incredible and over-the-top as Satan's temptations of Jesus were, they were all cheap tricks that used the extreme to tempt Jesus to question what he knew about God. His response? Jesus answered, "It is said: 'Do not put the Lord your God to the test'" (Luke 4:12).

Jesus' response is quite profound. As with all of his individual responses to the temptations, Jesus is quoting from the Old Testament. This particular quote is from Deuteronomy 6:16 which references an incident that happens in Exodus chapter 17. In the passage in Exodus, the people are getting thirsty, and in those extreme circumstances they question whether or not God is going to provide for them. The problem is that they know the answer to whether or not God will provide for them. They had all witnessed the waters turning to blood, the boils on people's skin, the plague of the firstborn from which they were spared, and all other of the ten plagues. They had all been there as they walked out of Egypt and crossed a parted Red Sea only to have it fall back on Pharaoh's army. More than anyone else, they knew about God's provision, yet they allowed some extreme circumstance to cause them to doubt it.

This method of using extreme circumstances to have people doubt their God is a common theme in the Bible, and we should take Jesus' council seriously: don't do it! This is not a tactic that should be in our playbook.

Grace in Justification

For those who are in the stream of the Christian faith mapped out by John Wesley, we have a different approach. As I mentioned in the last chapter, we believe that there are several forms of God's grace that are extended to the world. When we are talking about salvation, we are talking about the form known as justifying grace. This is the grace by which we are cleansed of our sin and are born into the body of Christ (this is the meaning of the "second birth" or being "born again").

The whole thing is Salvation [handwritten margin note]

To be clear, this is not something we do for ourselves. It is something that God chooses to do for us, and anyone who allows God's prevenient grace to bring them to the point of being ready to follow Jesus will receive the fullness of this grace as a gift from God.

What Wesley recognized was that this was not some mechanical process. Rather, each person would come to this point from a different path and his or her response to the justifying grace of God would have its own unique form. Because this is such an abstract, mystical experience, we can be tempted to cheapen it into a couple of belief statements and a prayer, but that is not the course ahead of us.

Walls and Centers

I believe Wesley's understanding of justification may best be understood visually through a concept laid out by Michael Frost and Alan Hirsch. They talk about faith in terms of a bounded set and centered set. Bounded-set Christianity can be drawn as a box with a cross in the

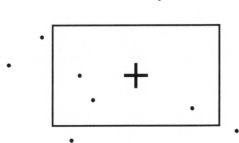

center. That box is what marks out the "line of faith" the evangelist was talking about in my friend's fellowship hall. In this approach, a lot of time and energy is spent on making sure the location, size, and every detail of the line are as clear as possible.

The goal of the people inside the box is also clear: get people to cross the line of faith. This approach is great in its focus on evangelism and getting as many people in heaven as possible, but it loses its focus on its true center. The real problem is encountered once people cross the line. Now that they are in, what are they to do? Because so much time is spent defining and refining the edge, the center is fuzzy. In this system, though Jesus is impor-tant, he is most important in the ways that he describes and clarifies the line and the method for crossing it. That means that once people are in, they concentrate on learning the things about Jesus that can help them get more people to cross the line.

The centered set removes the line and places the cross at the center with a tight circle around it. The main focus here is to clarify the person of Jesus. Rather than each individual seeing themselves in relation to which side of the line they are on, they see themselves in relation to the person of Jesus. Because of the clarity of his position, they can see how far they are from him and their motion in relationship to him. (Are they moving toward or away from?) The goal in this system is to lift Jesus up, point him out to everyone, and encourage each person to turn their lives and follow him.

This is the kind of justification Wesley spoke about. Rather than a cookie-cutter method, this leaves room for a "way" of salvation with individual nuance. With Jesus lifted up at the center of our life and world, everyone is

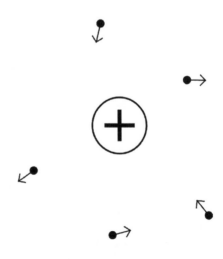

presented with the ability to see their life in relation to him. Each individual, then, has an opportunity to turn his or her life and follow him or not.

That turning can look different for different people. For some, they turn degree by degree over many years until one day they discover that their choices have led them to the place where they have decided to follow Jesus. For others, there are "about-face" moments when a friend or pastor taps them on the shoulder to point out the loving Savior that has been beckoning them from behind for years and they decide to turn in a moment of intense emotion. There are those two and as many other options as there are people—the key is repentance: turning and following Jesus. When we decide to let go and turn, God's grace overflows. He forgives our sins and brings us into the body of Christ. Though our sin carries with it the punishment of a broken relationship with God, justifying grace offers to remove the sin and the guilt it carries with it.

But how do you know? How do you *know* that you know that you're saved? That was an issue that plagued Wesley for his entire life. He called it receiving the assurance of salvation, and waited for a long time before he received it. Wesley wanted a faith that a man could have without knowing that he had it. His heart longed to know that everything about him had changed because of the Holy Spirit's coming. How did the assurance of salvation manifest itself in Wesley's life? It happened when he stopped into a small-group gathering one night on Aldersgate Street. While someone read from a Bible commentary, John felt his heart strangely warmed and was sure that he was saved.

Glimpses of Justifying Grace in the Bible

Some make the erroneous assumption that God's justifying grace makes its first appearance with Jesus, but that is far from the reality. One verse that proclaims God's grace comes from the Old Testament in 2 Chronicles 7:14, "If my people, who are called by my name, will humble themselves and pray and seek my face and turn from their wicked ways, then I will hear from heaven, and I will forgive their sin and will heal their land." One of the more interesting things this verse reveals about justifying grace is that it extends beyond the individual. God wants to set the *whole world* right again, which means that part of this form of his grace is the way in which he uses his people who are following him to bring about the redemption of the world. (More on that in chapter 5.)

First John uses a cleansing metaphor to describe this grace saying, "If we confess our sins, he is faithful and just and will forgive us our sins and purify us from all unrighteousness" (1:9). This verse reveals that justifying grace is like washing clothes. Though all you have to bring is dirty laundry, all you have to do is hand it over and God takes care of making it new again.

Jesus talks about this form of grace to a Pharisee named Nicodemus in John 3. He speaks of its role in bringing us into a new family (called by Paul the body of Christ). Jesus says that one must be born again into this new family. How does this happen? Jesus explains it in Old Testament terms saying, "Just as Moses lifted up the snake in the wilderness, so the Son of Man must be lifted up, that everyone who believes may have eternal life in him" (John 3:14–15).

Justifying Moment

"God has been telling a story since the beginning of creation, since before you were born. He sent his son to repair the brokenness created by our sin, and has come to you today—wherever you are, however far you are from him. And he asks us one question. He asks us all the same question: Will you follow me?" That was the plea at the winter retreat. After struggling with how to deal with salvation, rededication, and all that other -ations I had received from my youth-ministry past, I arrived here on the last night of the retreat.

We had traced the story of God through creation, the fall, and Jesus, being clear about who everyone was, why everything had happened, and most important of all, how it explained our world right then. Though we had response times to consider who we were, and where we were in relation to God, there was no offer for justification. The room was ready for it.

When I walked out onto the stage it was as if everyone (the lifelong Christians and the friends who had been on the edge of our ministry for a while) was poised to jump up and respond. When they responded and kneeled to pray together, it was something particularly beautiful to me. There wasn't one group that was just walking in to the house of faith, nor was there another full of people who had somehow slipped out the back door and were making their way back on the inside. There wasn't even a group of people who were on the inside of the walls of faith helping people over the threshold. There was Jesus, and all of us, together, turning to follow him from where we were. There was justifying grace redeeming us all and providing salvation and inclusion in the incredible gift of the body of Christ.

Justifying Ministry

As with everything else, this understanding of God and how he works in the world helps us decide how our ministries should look and what we should do. We talked about the ministries that seek to convey the prevenient grace of God as being those that have a significant percentage of non-group attendees. Justifying-grace ministries should be seen as a logical next step for students who have come to those prevenient events, as well as an important part of the life of those who have been around for a while. The goal here is to create an environment conducive to students seeing themselves in relation to Jesus and choosing to turn (or re-turn) and follow him.

That's right, I said re-turn. A common issue people have with focusing a program on this justifying grace theme is, "What about the students who are already Christians?" The response is that God is offering his justifying grace to them as well. Many who made commitments in the past have chosen to turn away, and need to turn again to a life that follows Jesus.

This all sounds cut and dried, but the reality is that when we talk about justifying grace and salvation we are talking about a process that is a continual seamless flow from not following to following. It is common for people to gradually be turning their lives toward Jesus as they consider faith. Through God's prevenient grace we described in the chapter before, they are wooed toward God bit by bit. When offered an opportunity to formally commit themselves to following Jesus, people in this state can find that it is a mere formality as they have already begun to follow him over time.

Camps and retreats have been a common setting for this type of ministry in the past. Part of the reason for their success in conveying the justifying grace of God is the amount of continuous or connected time available. This attribute of the camp setting gives time to go through the entire process in one event. The extended time also helps overcome developmental hurdles as students are at various levels of psychological maturity, which means that any one of the mental tasks in this process may take time for them to complete. At a camp or retreat you generally have four or more hours of instruction time and extra time available for conversation that help hold students' hands and walk with them along this process.

That is the important task for justifying ministries: the process. No matter what the theme is, the process should be the same. Let's look at each piece of that process.

Describing God and Jesus. You choose the lens. You can use a series of gross stories in the Bible; station-based worship on art and beauty; small conversation clusters around current issues; or any other wild, engaging idea your team can develop to get the message out. What is important is that we make clear who Jesus is and the life he demonstrated for us to live.

Students locate their life in relation to Jesus. Method aside, after firmly planting the person (location) of Jesus, students are given prompts to consider their own life by setting their own theoretical location: Who are they?

What do they believe? How do they live? Then, and this is the important part, they are asked to hold their life up against some standard or teaching of Jesus.

Students determine the direction of their life in relation to Jesus. This is a process issue. Determining a trajectory requires students to think about the recent past, and then use that to forecast the future. This is not about asking them to do the impossible task of figuring out where they will be in five years, but asking them to decide whether or not they are heading toward Jesus.

Students are given the opportunity to turn to Jesus. Few students will find that they are headed in a 100 percent right direction. That means some need a minor course correction, while others need to turn 180 degrees. The important element here is the opportunity being presented in a way that is respectful of the power of the Holy Spirit to bring repentance *and* open to the many ways students might need to express such turning. While one might need to kneel at an altar, another might need to pour their hearts out to a volunteer. Regardless of the method, it is important to offer students an opportunity to make decisions and have defining moments in their faith journey.

Welcome to Struggleville: Next stop, the New Jerusalem. Leaving it there does the students a disservice, as the Christian life is full of struggle, both against personal temptation and evil as well as societal evil and structures of injustice. This is the moment to introduce the ideas connected to sanctifying grace (more on that in the next chapter) and focus the life of the Christian through the Great Commission to the New Jerusalem—heaven on earth where God rules and there is no more crying or pain. Our goal is to go into the world and make earth look more like that. We do that personally through personal holiness and corporately through mission, service, and discipleship.

Justifying Ministers

As ridiculous as it may sound to say that Jesus needs to be the focus of your energy and ministry, I find that too often, my focus slips onto something else. Don't get me wrong, they are all good things like designing an excellent discipleship process or a creative environment for a retreat or dealing with a string of crises in the group, but as good as they can be, they can all be a distraction from Jesus.

As a pastor, I need to be constantly concerned with introducing people to Jesus by finding engaging ways to show him off that give clarity to his life. I need to teach with the idea that, at some point, Jesus will make the same call on everyone's life: follow me.

A brilliant theologian named Parker Palmer talked about the method behind making that introduction in his book *To Know as We Are Known*. He said our role is to let go of our need to be seen as the authority. We need to let go of our need to be the focus of our ministries and teaching moments. We need to try our best to be a third party that is helping our people meet and explore our subject matter. We want to give that subject matter a life and personality outside our own that honors the reality of the content. This is never more important than when we are talking about Jesus and the Scripture. We need to resist the temptation to remake Jesus in our image; instead, we need to point to the places where Jesus disagrees with us, where he challenges us, and how his life is the key to understanding our life and making sense of our world.

Though we do not need to ask everyone to bow their head and raise their hand if they want to follow Jesus, we do not need to be afraid to give voice to the call of Jesus to follow him. When the groundwork has been laid, it is nothing short of totally irresponsible to stop short of, to use a sales term, "making the ask."

How would your ministry change if you paid attention to where students were in their process of faith? What would happen if you started asking students to locate themselves in relation to the Jesus they had met through your teaching? What if you made a point to offer the justifying grace of God to students who were beginning to make the turn in their life?

➡ Personal Processing:

1. Think of a recent conversation with a student who you feel is not following Jesus but has been at least checking things out for a while. How did you do focusing on the aspects of justifying grace described in this chapter? Did you consider trying to identify where he or she was in the process?

2. Make a list of three students you should have the conversation with and when/how you might be able to accomplish it.

3. What would you have to do to make the conversation spiritual but not pushy? How could you communicate care rather than persuasion? How far along in the process could you imagine walking with each student in one conversation?

4. How will you discern whether or not the student is ready for you to "make the ask"?

→ Ministry/Team Processing

1. Make a list of all your ministries that have a significant percentage of students present who have been part of your church or have been checking things out for a while.

2. Of those ministries, which are (or should be) focused on conveying justifying grace?

3. Take each ministry and write down each of its major components.

4. Now it's evaluation time. Look at each component and ask: Does this do a good job of conveying justifying grace? Which part of the process does each portion cover? Are there any parts of the process missing?

5. Take a moment to discuss with your team how the personal processing challenged you. What is one thing you want to change or do differently as a result?

3

Holy Sunday School!

(Sanctifying Grace in Awkward Silence)

I am ready to give you one hundred candy bars." The passionate preacher unveiled what looked like two hundred boxes of Hershey bars. I was getting excited. "You can have one, but they aren't all for you. I want you to enjoy yours, and then bless other people with the same gift I gave you." Less cool, but I was ready.

I was at an evangelism training–focused youth conference that was in our town trying to help us "take back our city for Jesus." I was thinking that things were getting off to a great start. This candy-giving technique could be a good way to get them to come to church.

"How long do you think it would take to give them away? Or how about this: If I gave you one hundred candy bars, how long would it take you to get ten people to give away some of those candy bars to their friends? Why is it so much easier to give away candy bars than talk to people about Jesus? Why is it so hard to get your friends . . . your *Christian* friends to help you do it? If you believe that Jesus is better than a candy bar, how many people have you talked about Jesus with this week?"

Wow . . . I was blown away. Jesus was *way* more important than candy, but I hadn't told anyone about him that week. I hadn't told anyone about him in a long time!

"That is what it means to be a Christian. Jesus tells us to go and tell the whole world about him." He started reading some verse about being sent out but I was sinking into conviction about my lack of being a real Christian. This whole time I hadn't been doing the main thing Jesus told me to do. Today was going to be the last day of that.

The speaker went into a method for talking to random strangers about Jesus. There was an opening question about if they cared about what happened when they died, which ultimately led to asking if they'd like to pray to accept Jesus. Then they released us on our local mall in pairs as a trial. We came back afterward and shared our experiences of being shunned, criticized—and of one person actually praying with someone to receive Christ! It was worth it!

Then, to the beach, where we were told to look for people who might be inebriated, as they were more receptive to the gospel! And they threw in a new twist; we each had a box of those candy bars.

• • •

Candy-Bar Faith

This myopic version of what it means to be a Christian is just about as unhealthy for your spirit as a candy bar is for your body. This minster was teaching exactly what we introduced in the last chapter. When you have a bounded-set view of faith, it becomes about the boundaries instead of the center. This "fuzzy center" we talked about in the previous chapter is where the real focus should be.

Though evangelism is important, it is not the only focus of our faith, and it is far more nuanced than giving away candy bars. In fact, sitting in the room listening to that preacher/trainer, there was no talk of what I should be doing with my life other than getting more and more people into heaven.

That weekend, I prayed with a couple of people to receive Jesus, and told them afterwards that they needed to walk their friends through the tract we gave them so that they could go to heaven too.

Praying with them was a rush that lasted for a while. However, just as you crash after eating too many candy bars, I came down hard after that weekend because when I got home I had no idea why I was doing all that. Sure, going to heaven was great, but it seemed to be lacking in the whole eternal-life-right-now department.

I opened up the Bible study they gave us and found more of the same. The study was an expanded version of the method we were using to take back our city for Jesus, complete with verses to memorize that would help us be better evangelists. So, I went to my youth pastor and asked him what he thought of all that, and he showed me the thread that, once pulled, unraveled the veil that was hiding the true power and full life I needed: holiness.

Sanctifying Grace, Power, and Perfection

My youth pastor was hopelessly uncool in a good way. He didn't try to dress things up, but was simple and direct.

He said that what I was missing was a focus on becoming more and more like Jesus. It was exactly what I needed to hear. It was what I was hungering for, and it was just about the least cool response he could have given. Thank God he wanted to be my pastor instead of my friend.

This is the next form of grace for us: sanctifying grace. Simply put, sanctifying grace is the grace of God that calls us and empowers us to be more than we are. Though we are forgiven when we choose to follow Jesus, we are not rid of every sinful tendency (a fact that is familiar to every Christian). No amount of self-help or personal actualization will rid us of this tendency. We simply do not have the power within us to become like Christ.

One thing is for sure: God does not call us to do something that he does not empower us to do. That power is sanctifying grace. It is both what convicts us of our sin and gives us the resources beyond our natural ability to let go of the sin that entangles us and live lives of victory and holiness. It is the mystical power of the holy love of God filling us and unleashing within us the image of God.

The goal is to surrender our heart to the power of the love of the Spirit, and allow it to radiate out from that surrendered center to consume every inch of our life until we are perfected in love.

This goal of being like Jesus feels on its surface to be unattainable, fantastic hyperbole. The goal is perfection. The initial response to this is almost always, "There is no one perfect except Jesus!" However, the perfection we are talking about is a specific brand. It has two defining aspects that bring it within reach. First, we need to understand that Christian perfection is the cessation of *intentional* sin. This is not the accidental stuff we do or the unintentional mistakes that happen, but choosing to sin. It's still a tall order, but at least something that seems a bit more realistic.

The second defining aspect is best told through the story of an early Methodist, and friend of John Wesley, named John Fletcher. He was an incredible figure not only in the leadership of the early movement in England, but a brilliant mind who helped hone Wesley's teaching into concise theology, publishing several works laying it out in clear, thorough language.

A friend of Fletcher explained that he was at a gathering of believers one evening when Fletcher made an announcement: he had received Christian perfection. As un-humble as that sounds, he continued, saying that he had received it twice before but felt that he lost it because he was being falsely humble. He had refrained from telling others for fear that they might think him arrogant. Since it was obvious that this was not something that could be attained of one's own effort, he said his silence meant that the Holy Spirit was not getting credit for the work that the Spirit had accomplished in him.

That brings us to the second defining aspect of perfection: it is not permanent. It means that we are to seek to receive from God the ability to not intentionally sin, and if we are not careful, we will lose it by intentionally sinning. That is far more accessible than it seems on the face of it, and definitely something worth seeking.

Glimpses of Sanctifying Grace in the Bible

This call of God on our lives to be more than we are is seen throughout the Old Testament in the words of the prophets constantly calling out to the people on behalf of God. They say things like Jeremiah did, calling out for repentance, "Perhaps when the people of Judah hear about every disaster I plan to inflict on them, they will each turn from their wicked ways; then I will forgive their wickedness and their sin" (Jer. 36:3).

It is a huge part of Jesus' teachings as well. In the Sermon on the Mount, when he talks about love, he is quick to point out that there is a measure of love that even people who are not following him express. He says, "If you love those who love you, what reward will you get? Are not even the tax collectors doing that? And if you greet only your own people, what are you doing more than others? Do not even pagans do that?" (Matt. 5:46–47). That passage serves to illustrate two concepts. First, there is some level of holiness and "being a good person" that is available to anyone who can exhibit the human trait of self-control. However, we are called to more, a fact that he makes quite clear in the very next verse: "Be perfect, therefore, as your heavenly Father is perfect" (Matt. 5:48). Though it is arguable that Jesus is using hyperbole here, the fact remains that he is encouraging the disciples to live beyond what they are capable of themselves.

Another key passage is in 1 John chapter 3. It speaks of the fact that the goal of Jesus was to destroy the works of the devil, and points out that "No one who is born of God will continue to sin, because God's seed remains in them; they cannot go on sinning, because they have been born of God" (v. 9). Strong words. But they under-score the point that our goal is to let go of all the places we are holding back, all the parts of our life we keep for ourselves, and all our little pet sins. If we do that, if we will allow the grace of God to take control of every single part of who we are, we will be unable to sin because our surrender has allowed the Holy Spirit to transform us into the "new creation" we long to become.

Sanctifying Moment

The problem is that our world is full of objects and values that serve as a constant distraction. Fighting through all of that to hear the voice of the Spirit calling us to holiness can be almost impossible at times. To help our students with this, we planned a silence and solitude retreat where we took a break from everything electronic for twenty-four hours and spent time praying and listening to God.

The retreat orbited around exploring several ancient prayer practices. We offered a teaching about the practice and then gave the students at least thirty minutes to explore the practice for themselves. After the prayer time was finished, we came back together to share our experiences.

One of the most affecting practices we explored was something called *Lectio Divina*. This prayer method uses a laser-focus on the Scripture to listen to God. As you read a passage over and over, you pay attention to what part might be the passage God wants to use to speak, then through careful focus on the passage, you pay attention to God's voice and rest in his presence. It is as simple to understand as it is powerful to experience.

After leading students through a demonstration, we let them go for half an hour to listen. When they returned, they were full of stories about God revealing difficult places and sensitive areas of weakness. They told stories of being filled with the love of God and experiencing true transformation at the hands of God's Word. They had a profound encounter with the sanctifying grace of God.

Sanctifying Ministry

Maybe you can concede the possibility of this brand of Christian perfection, but without some practical pieces it stays in the realm of theory. Luckily, Wesley was intensely practical (his movement was nicknamed "Methodist," after all).

In his sermon "Scripture Way of Salvation," he gives a nice list of ways in which this grace is received: "First, all works of piety; such as public prayer, family prayer, and praying in our closet; receiving the supper of the Lord; searching the Scriptures, by hearing, reading, meditating; and using such a measure of fasting or abstinence as our bodily health allows." Those are the practices Wesley saw as imparting the sanctifying grace of God.

We've been steadily moving through different groups of people within your youth ministry, and now are talking about ministry that focuses on those that have committed their lives to Jesus and have decided to follow him. That means that the programs that are primarily made up of those committed teens are the ones best suited for focusing on communicating this form of God's grace. Though all churches are different, my experience has been that the students who will wake up early on a Sunday morning and come to more than just worship (i.e., Sunday school) generally are those committed Christians that are seeking to live more holy lives.

In addition to reaching this more committed group of students, the Sunday school model has lent itself to one of the means of grace: the searching of the Scriptures. (More on the means of grace in chapter 8.) With some tweaks, many of the Sunday school classes would be great opportunities for people to experience the sanctifying grace of God.

One of the defining attributes of this "searching" approach to Scripture is that it is active. Unfortunately, most studies and curricula have devolved into a passive receipt of propositional knowledge. While this is a good place to begin, in order to experience the grace of God, we have to break out of that mold and become active participants in this searching. That means that when structuring these classes and selecting curricula, we must look for and provide time for meditation and action.

Most curriculum have some sort of section that is called "application" that usually consists of a set of questions about how this could be lived out in your life, but meditation is really the next level. Meditation is opening up to the inspiration of the Spirit to make those profound connections between God's Word and our reality. This is what I call allowing the Scripture to "read us." It begins with being willing to sit in silence as we consider concepts deeply and listen to the leading of the Spirit before we give voice to insight.

This can be difficult especially because our society is unhealthily uncomfortable with silence, but we must let go of our desire to fill the silence with our surface-level reflexive reactions to what has been discovered and discussed. For some it may even require imposing some artificial time before which people are not allowed to answer. It is through these sorts of techniques that we reveal the power of making space to hear the Spirit.

Once we have received from the Spirit, it is time to put our knowledge into action. Rather than discussing hypothetical ways in which this can impact our lives, we must look at first steps that we can take in the room or soon after we leave to live out the call of the Scriptures in our lives.

Searching Scripture is not the only means Wesley discusses. Another he mentions is the practice of public prayer. Helping Christians become comfortable with public prayer is an important aspect of these ministries as well. Far from practicing public-speaking skills, this is part of the way God moves through a community in the life of individuals. There are as many methods for doing this as there are teachers willing to challenge their classes to do it.

The key is to raise the bar of participation and lower the bar of expectation. By that, I mean everyone should be challenged to participate while the leader should do everything to let them know that all offerings are beautiful to God, no matter how short or disjointed they are. If we will commit to remaking our ministries with a focus on these means of God's sanctifying grace, we can open our people up to the transformation it offers.

All of this practicality is helpful, but can make this brilliant gift of God out to be a little self-helpy. So, let's be clear. Sanctifying grace is not some magical motivational method to help you break bad habits and start good ones. It is not a new (old) way to justify legalism and judgmentalism. Sanctifying grace is a person captured by God. It is the deep longing within us to surrender our lives fully to a loving Savior, and it is a power beyond ourselves to truly experience and express the love of a holy God. It is a mystical, divine union whereby many very practical observable traits are transformed.

Sanctifying Ministers

Luckily, attaining this ideal of "entire sanctification" is not a prerequisite to becoming a pastor. However, I believe that our lack of ability to stop intentionally sinning causes us to stop short of teaching this to others. Don't get me wrong, not wanting to be a hypocrite is a good thing, but there are ways to talk about sanctification that do not turn us into pompous Pharisees. And it begins with the recognition that it is not about us getting better at self-control. Sanctifying grace is about us getting better at surrendering to the love of the Holy Spirit and allowing it to give us the supernatural power of change.

Even with this clear understanding, we need to be careful in how we communicate this gift. We start with what the sanctifying grace of God brings into clearest focus: our weakness. We begin by recognizing our weakness to temptation, our inability to fully free ourselves from the bonds of sin, and use that sense of futility to lead into this gift of grace. The sanctifying grace of God not only helps us to see where it is that we need to turn from our sin, but—if we will allow it—will give us the strength we need to let go of sin and receive all the gifts that the obedient life affords us.

Though entire sanctification can be held up as a goal, as something to constantly be striving toward, the bulk of our communication should be on the 99 percent of people who have not yet attained it. The main way we deliver this wonderful news of God empowering us to live lives of obedience, is to treat it positively rather than negatively.

Too often we buy into the culture's lie that sin is good and letting go of it is bad, difficult, or undesirable. We phrase our teaching in terms of "the hard climb up the hill" or "it's worth it." The reality is that sin is negative, evil, and destructive. Though it may have some temporary enjoyment associated with it, it is not good. It is hurting us, and conceding anything less is a lie.

Letting go of sin has almost nothing but upside. When done with humility and transparency, it can lead others to the same thing. In addition, there is nothing quite like being used by God. There is nothing quite like the incredible gift of living your life obedient to God's call.

Did you notice the error I made here? I have yet to talk about striving after sanctification myself, in favor of talking about how to communicate it. That is our common pattern. How often do we spend our time and energy finding great packaging for theological truth, finding the perfect pitch for this amazing product, and neglect our own spiritual development?

Do you want to know the best way to learn how to communicate the power of God's sanctifying grace? Want to know the best way to conceptualize it so that you can communicate it? Live it yourself. I believe that as we surrender our life to God and let go of sin, we will discover the profound blessing it is. Then, armed with this firsthand knowledge, we can communicate it to the souls God has placed in our care.

→ **Personal Processing**

1. Take a moment to open yourself up to the probing of the Holy Spirit. Are you pursuing holiness in every way possible? Where are your weak areas? If they are simple, how can you move quickly toward holiness? If they are more difficult, or longer-term struggles, whom can you enlist to help you?

2. When was the last time that you had a relatively deep conversation with a student who was a committed Christian? How did you do focusing on the aspects of sanctifying grace as described in this chapter? If you steered clear of sin or holiness, why?

3. A one-on-one conversation about this kind of stuff is easiest to begin and most well received when you have a deeper relationship with a student. Make a list of three students you have a deeper relationship with and when you will schedule a time to hang out and talk about grace.

4. How could you get into a conversation about where they are struggling and how they could make steps toward holiness in those areas?

5. How are you doing on utilizing all the means of grace? What areas of your life could you work them into what you are already doing?

➡ Ministry/Team Processing

1. Make a list of all your ministries that have a significant percentage of students present who are committed Christians.

2. Of those ministries, which are (or should be) focused on conveying sanctifying grace?

3. Take each ministry and write down each of its major components.

4. Now it's evaluation time. Look at each component and ask: Does this do a good job of conveying sanctifying grace? Which means of grace is used? Would another means of grace be better?

5. Take a moment to discuss with your team how the personal processing challenged you. What is one thing you want to change or do differently as a result?

Part Two

Reclaiming Salvation—A Lifelong Workshop

"Everyone, though born of God in an instant, yet undoubtedly grows by slow degrees."

—John Wesley,

Letter 27, June 1760

4

Youth Worship Channel

(The Means of Grace Unplugged)

My hands were shaking a little bit as I walked up to the imposing facade of the big church in town. I was going to my first after-school Christian club worship meeting of my high school career. My nervousness did not subside when I entered the building. It was just like the lunchroom at school. It was full of people I didn't know and all gathered into their predetermined cliques. Over in the corner closest to the pizza was most of the football team (they were unofficially required to come by their coach); not too far off were their cheerleader girlfriends; and on the other side was half of the marching band. I got some pizza, found a couple of friends, and waited until we were ushered into the youth room.

It began with a weird sort of practical joke where a visitor was sent out of the room and they made what appeared to be a three-seat-long couch by placing two chairs about a chair's width apart, covering the whole setup with a sheet and having two of the cheerleaders sit on the chairs. The visitor was brought back in and asked to give his best pickup line to the cheerleaders, who offered him a seat in between them in the empty space hidden by the sheet. When he sat down, the girls stood up and the crowd erupted in laughter.

There were a couple more games that were a little less humiliating, followed up with a band that played all the right songs from camp and a couple of secular love-song covers that sounded like they could have a spiritual double meaning. By the end of the performance I was pretty sure that the lead singer had hooked two of the four girls that were standing in front of him staring bleary-eyed at his high school rock-star clothing and moves.

After that, there was a skit that I had seen a couple of weeks before on *Saturday Night Live*, which led somewhat awkwardly into the final act: the coach/speaker. He walked up with a Bible that was *way* more worn out than mine, and walked us through the four spiritual laws. I wasn't sure why, but having someone preach at that point felt totally out of place. After his talk that was way longer than he had claimed it would be at the beginning, with every head bowed and eye closed, he asked those of us who wanted to be saved to raise our hands.

"There are hands going up all over the room," he exclaimed much to my surprise. I couldn't help myself. I figured I was concealed enough by the darkness of the back row to not be worried about getting caught peeking. I was as enraged as I was heartbroken. As he repeated some version of "I see that hand," I scanned the crowd. There were no hands. Not a single one was going up even though this creep at the front was saying there was.

I left during the closing prayer, not sure what to do. When I got home one of my friends who was there called me on the phone. When I answered, the first words out of his mouth were, "that was weird." We talked for a while, trying to figure it out, and we came to the conclusion that it felt like someone had added a dose of spirituality to an above-average high school party. We weren't sure how Christian club worship should be done, but this was not it.

• • •

Lying on Jesus' Behalf

I know. With so much brokenness, where do we begin? Do we dive into the humiliation of people considering becoming a part of Jesus' community or the co-opting of worship music to get a date, or the outright lies used to close the "worship" service? Though I never experienced all of this at the same service again, I've been consistently amazed as I have seen all the elements recur throughout my life as a Christian.

After years of reflection on this and similar events, I believe that all of the weird elements of this service tie into the same fundamental misunderstanding: the particulars of what we do aren't really important. But, actions do matter! The specific things we do in the worship service matter. They matter way more than we may realize at first because they are the means by which God is conveying his grace to those in attendance.

Too often the focus of youth programs is on getting laughs, making people cry, or keeping the attention of everyone there. What the students who planned all the creative and fun elements of my traumatic experience didn't consider was: How is this going to communicate the grace of God? In fact they might have done well to ask, "Is this skit, game, etc., going to elicit emotions and portray truths that are in direct opposition to the grace of God?"

It is not surprising that the message felt out of place and that there was no one responding. However, the actions of the leader in the front of the room—lying on Jesus' behalf—crossed way over the line. Whether it was an ego problem or a genuine attempt to help students feel it was okay to make a decision because others were doing the same, it was a lie. It was a lie about the work of the Holy Spirit, and that is the kind of lie that makes Christianity look fake. That is the kind of lie that makes believers doubt and doubters leave.

The Means of Grace

Every piece of the Christian life is about the grace of God in some way or another, but the question that we touched upon in chapter 3 is, "How do we receive that grace?" John Wesley said there are several different means by which we receive the grace of God. He described them as the outward signs, words, or actions that serve as the channel for God to give preventing, justifying, and sanctifying grace.[2]

The most important distinction to be made here is that these practices are a *means* of grace. They are not the point of the Christian life. They are the way by which we reach the point of the Christian life: God's grace. The reason that is important is because if these means of grace are seen as an end in themselves they lose their power. When they are not done in order to receive God's grace, they become the dead implements of religion that are as lifeless as they are pointless. John Wesley described this focusing on the means as an end as having the form of religion but lacking its power.[3]

All of this is to underscore that in order for these means of grace to fulfill their purpose, they must constantly be pointing the believer beyond the practice itself to something greater. At this point it is important to note that it was a commitment to the means of grace that was a defining aspect of the movement begun by Wesley. Though they are not to be our focus in themselves, they are to be our focus as paths toward our desired end, and neglecting them is neglecting our relationship with God. So, what are they? The means of grace are normally divided into two categories: acts of piety and acts of mercy.

The acts of piety are those things that people most often think of when we begin the discussing how we grow closer to God. They are the first answers in most Sunday school classes and are the focus of much of the typical ministry of the church. Though historians debate the specifics of the list, most agree at least on prayer, fasting, searching the Scriptures, communion, and conferencing (meeting together with Christians).

These were not occasional practices, but woven into the fabric of all aspects of life and served to maintain a constant awareness of the presence and grace of God in the life of the believer. People were to spend time every day in prayer and searching the Scriptures, fast once a week as their body allowed, receive communion once a week, and gather with Christians several times a week.

The second category, acts of mercy, is not always at the front of people's minds when they consider how it is that they experience God's grace in their life. The works of mercy are feeding the hungry, clothing the naked, entertaining the stranger, visiting people who are sick or in prison or deficient in some other way as in the case of ignorance. For Wesley, these are just as full a means of grace as fasting and prayer. In other words, you will receive as much of the grace of God by praying as you will by visiting prisoners. In fact, Wesley argued that the acts of mercy were greater than those of piety because not only does the believer receive the grace of God as they do when they are engaging in an act of piety, but the person being served (prisoner, naked, sick) also receives the grace of God.

This is why the movements that have grown from the theology of John Wesley are known for their work in the world. It is why a large percentage of the schools and hospitals in the United States were started by people seeking to give and receive God's grace. It is why our ministries need to be focused on more than teaching the Bible and singing worship songs.

Glimpses of the Means of Grace in the Scripture

Every one of the means of grace has a long list of Scriptures from which it is derived and each one of those means of grace deserves a study of its own. So, we are going to take a step back and look at some of the broader ideas connected to the means of grace in the Scriptures.

One of the deepest concepts expressed by the means of grace is that what we do matters. Since the beginning, God has provided a framework for both how we live and how we worship. That idea can be found in one of the most important passages in the Scripture for the Jewish people called the *Shema* in Deuteronomy 6:4–9. Many of the Jewish people throughout the ages have recited it every day before they got out of bed and at night before their head hit the pillow. It says:

> "Hear, O Israel: The LORD our God, the LORD is one. Love the LORD your God with all your heart and with all your soul and with all your strength. These commandments that I give you today are to be on your hearts. Impress them on your children. Talk about them when you sit at home and when you walk along the road, when you lie down and when you get up. Tie them as symbols on your hands and bind them on your foreheads. Write them on the doorframes of your houses and on your gates."

We often think of this passage as talking about the Bible, and though that interpretation is valid, in its original context, it was talking about the laws contained at least in the book of Deuteronomy and most likely in the entire Torah. If you read on in Deuteronomy, you will find instructions from God on what to do with the inhabitants when a region is conquered (chap. 7), which foods are considered clean (chap. 14), what is required to convict someone of a crime (chap. 19), and how to deal with a rebellious son (chap. 21). If there is one thing that all that detail communicates, it is: *how* we do what we do matters to God. He wants to fill our lives with his presence. He not only wants to give us his grace, he wants to give us the means whereby we receive it.

The acts of piety do not represent any sort of innovation in theology. In fact, they connect to the most ancient parts of our faith. Since the earliest moments of the faith, people have been doing some elements of each of these spiritual practices. One of the earliest moments is the worship of Cain and Abel in Genesis 4. Much has been made of the difference between the offerings of Cain and Abel, many of them centering around the fact that Cain brought "some" of his crops while Abel brought the best. Regardless of what the reasoning was behind the acceptance and rejection of the offerings, two points are clear: God wants us to connect with him, and he wants us to do so in specific ways. Those ways have remained fairly consistent throughout the millennia, and are summarized in the acts of piety.

You may have recognized the list of the acts of mercy as coming from a particularly interesting passage in the New Testament. Those acts come from Jesus' teaching about the sheep and the goats in Matthew 25. To those who did the acts of mercy, he says, "Come, you who are blessed by my Father; take your inheritance, the kingdom prepared for you since the creation of the world" (v. 34b). To those who did not do the acts of mercy, Jesus says, "Depart from me, you who are cursed, into the eternal fire prepared for the devil and his angels" (v. 41b). These are dramatic words that underscore the importance of a faith that reaches out to others and seeks to bring the kingdom of God more fully on earth. They convey a deep truth that the means of grace are bigger than the development of the individual, they are part of how God is making his will be done on earth as it is in heaven. These values strike at the center of all our faith practice, and have significant insights into how we do ministry and live as pastors.

Means-of-Grace Moment

We were in the thick of the right side of our brains. We were coming up with all kinds of ideas for how to make our next youth series rock. "Week four is about reaching out to those in need. Anyone have a great game or illustration that goes along with that?"

We had some incredibly horrible ideas. What about bingo with statistics of big problems? How about we have a guided meditation to help us imagine what it would be like to be in need? What if we made an outreach super-hero who jumped off the roof of the church while quoting that week's Scripture? (This guy is in every brainstorming meeting, right?) All of these were rescinded almost as soon as they were said—except for some intense conversation about the superhero BASE jumper.

Then, Peter raised his hand (something unheard of in this meeting), and I called on him. "Well,"—Peter tested the ground as he tiptoed into his idea—"you know, if we are talking about reaching others in need, I mean, it doesn't make a lot of sense to, you know, maybe we could, possibly, if it works out . . . What I'm trying to say is what good does talking about this do us? Why not just go help people?" In a single moment of clarity he had pulled back the curtains on our predilection to talk instead of act.

It was, of course, a no-brainer at that point. We were going to go help people that week and no amount of need for permission slips was going to stop us. We decided that we needed a song or two to get the last stragglers to arrive and then had the church vans cranked and ready to roll for the rest of our meeting time to work on various outreach work with those in need.

Means-of-Grace Ministry

When you look through the acts of piety and acts of mercy, nothing we do as individuals or organizations escapes the touch of the means of grace. If all our programs seek to convey the grace of God to those who are participants, the practical bits of exactly what happens in those settings matter as they become the channel through which that grace travels.

There is one setting in which many of these means of grace can come in the same program: worship. In the field of youth ministry it goes by different names. Some call it youth group or some acronym developed in the seventies or even some extreme, relevant name like "The Edge" or "The Well." Whatever you call it, the primary elements of this ministry are generally music and message. Some people add games or dramas, others download pricey videos to introduce their lesson, others still rock the overhead projector, but they all do the same thing: they come together to praise God and receive from him.

The deep truths about how God offers his grace to us (that actions matter, God wants us to connect with him and live out his will in the world) should shape every aspect of our worship (and every aspect of all our ministries). That means, first of all, that worship is not a time when we fly by the seat of our pants and decide what we are going to do and say thirty minutes before people arrive. This is a holy opportunity that deserves thought and prayer given to planning and preparation.

Because it is a moment in which we have the opportunity to engage with the grace of God, we do not do things that run contrary to that grace. It should go without saying that we don't do games like the couch game in which people are mocked, but the call of the means of the grace extends further than that. We should seek to create an overall environment in which people can experience the love of God from the moment they pull into the parking lot to the moment they pull back out and head home.

That environment shouldn't be externalized into some set of rules on a wall, but lived out in the lives of the leaders present, spoken about from the stage, and guarded with love when people move beyond its borders.

Worship represents an exciting opportunity to craft creative ways in which those present can both learn about the means of grace and experience them.

What if this week you teach about fasting and then call a fast for your group? You might even do a Wesley fast after the evening meal on Thursday to midafternoon on Friday (skipping breakfast and lunch) and text everyone who is participating devotional thoughts before they go to bed and when they rise during the fast.

If you are serious about making your worship an opportunity to engage in the means of grace, it will mean branching out of the more typical acts of piety into the acts of mercy as well. I was in a conference where the pastor of a large church in Detroit said that every once in a while he would surprise his people on Sunday morning and tell them that instead of a sermon, they were going to walk out of the church into the neighborhood and serve in one way or another. Then, the pastor would open the doors of the church and lead the way into the world. What a message!

What would it say if you got the church van gassed up and headed to a nursing home or hospital chapel for worship instead of your church next Sunday? What if you piled everyone into their cars and told them to go buy a couple of sandwiches and take them to the park and share a meal and conversation with the homeless who live there?

Those kinds of moments communicate volumes. Not only do they push people into doing acts of mercy that they may not normally do, but they also express to them that God's grace can come to them just as fully by visiting those in prison as it can from listening to an over-educated pastor talk about the Bible.

Means-of-Grace Ministers

If we aren't careful, all our training conferences and theology courses can cause us to forget an important truth: we are Christians before we are pastors. That means that we must be spending time engaging in the means of grace and growing closer to God. As easy as it can be to allow our faith to become professionalized and disappear from the private areas of our lives, we must guard against it. We must stay in love with the Scriptures, hunger for moments of prayer, and fight for victims of injustice. If not, we become the whitewashed tombs that Jesus talked about: we look good on the outside, but are full of death on the inside. In order to be effective as ministers, we must be vital Christians.

The means of grace has a lot to say about all of the trivial things we do and say when we are interacting with the people in our churches. The reality is that if you are a church leader, when you walk into a room, your presence is bigger than you. You walk into a room carrying the weight of your office as a leader. Your words and actions carry the significance of that role and color the people's understanding of faith in a more profound way than the average participant.

What you do matters. When you are telling inappropriate jokes or making fun of someone in the room, you are damaging far more than other people's opinion of you. As a representative of Jesus, you are cheapening the whole of Christianity. When you do not act as one who is seeking to be remade in the image of Christ, you are making the Christian life seem trivial, unimportant, or fake.

On the other extreme, if you are dressed in hypocritical perfection with a matching judgmental attitude, you do similar damage. People need to see that there is a struggle to the faith. It is not easy, and there is no need to make it look easy. We are all broken sinners and to pretend otherwise is just a lie. If you can be appropriately vulnerable, it gives people permission to continue to attempt to engage in the means of grace even when their propensity for sin causes them to fall flat or neglect them altogether.

With all that talk of the importance of our role in the room as faith leaders, the one thing that the means of grace make totally clear is that we are not the most significant piece of God's plan. All of the means of grace can be engaged without even having a minister at all. You do not need someone who knows how to read Greek to visit someone at the hospital. You do not need someone with graduate training in church history to be able to express your heart to God in a prayer. You definitely don't need someone who has had classes in worship theology and homiletics to engage in a fast. You don't even need to have someone who has been to a church leadership conference in order to search the Scriptures. God will use us if we surrender, but we are not the cornerstones in his plan.

All of that gives us a unique position in the church and the world. While we have a particular authority granted to our actions and words, God is clear that it is he that provides the grace and the channel through which it is given. We are humble guides and fellow travelers who move along those paths pointing to the real focus and keeping ourselves as low as possible so that God's grace can flow as freely as possible.

➜ Personal Processing

1. How are you doing on the means of grace? Do you carve out time to go to the local jail or tutor at the under-resourced school?

2. Look at your calendar and schedule some time in the upcoming couple of weeks to do one of the means of grace you have been neglecting.

3. Think about your words and actions when you are involved in programs and talking to parishioners. Are your words and actions reflecting the lifestyle of a person seeking to surrender to the Holy Spirit?

4. How are you at being appropriately vulnerable? Do you tend to give a more perfect persona? Do you over-share your faults and places you compromise morally? Take a moment to allow the Spirit to search your heart and reveal where adjustments need to be made.

➡ Ministry/Team Processing

1. Take a moment to list the means of grace, and then list the ministry expression of those means in your ministry.

2. Where are you overdoing it? Are there any means that are not being served in your current offerings? What changes need to be made to offer a balanced ministry?

3. Now look at your worship. What is your specific schedule? Is it conducive to exploring a diversity of the means of grace?

4. Take a moment to list common themes and activities. Are there favorite activities or creative elements?

5. Look over that list and mark which ones are moving with the means of grace. Are there any that are moving in the opposite direction?

6. Take a moment to discuss with your team how the personal processing challenged you. What is one thing you want to change or do differently as a result?

5

Visiting Small Groups

(Class Meetings on La-Z-Boys)

had been following Jesus for a while as a teenager when my friend told me that his church was starting something called "transformation groups." I had done a small group at my church, which had fizzled after a while, and I really missed it. The title of these groups sounded way better than "small"—after all, who cared about the size, I wanted "transformation."

We were supposed to bring our Bible and fifteen dollars to the first meeting, where I received a book that felt almost as heavy as my Bible. We talked about the book, and the requirements of the class. At each meeting we were going to go over all the information contained in the daily thirty-minute homework assignments in the book.

We concluded the time by praying over and signing a covenant, which began with the two main rules of the group: everything there was confidential, and if you didn't complete the homework, you were not allowed to speak each week.

I remember thinking this was going to be the level of intensity I needed to move to the next level in my relationship with God. The first week was less than perfect. I only was able to do about half of the assignments. Okay, about half of half of the assignments.

When I arrived, the teacher asked us to show our homework to a friend and then asked us to be honest: Did we finish the homework? About half of us did. The other half were silent until the prayer time. Next week, I did better and finished four. I was silent again. In fact, there was only one week of the times I attended where I was able to talk at all.

Needless to say, I was not nearly as transformed by the end of that group as I had hoped.

• • •

Soup-Nazi Small Groups

Book after book has been written about the difference in dynamics and potential for formation provided by getting people into small groups, but what I experienced was closer to *Seinfeld*'s Soup Nazi than what those books herald.

There were two main problems with the group. First, it was focused on study, which is not the same thing as focusing on transformation (as we will discover in a moment). All but a brief moment at the end was consumed with the dissemination and review of information.

And, if you were a normal teenager who was inconsistent with study, prone to procrastination, and lacking in study skills, the group leader said, "No soup for you!"

Despite the groups being named "transformation," they were really focused on learning a large body of information as well as developing consistency in doing deep study of Scripture. Both of those things could (and do) provide for transformation in the life of the believer, but by themselves are limited. Over and over again throughout church history, church leaders have discovered that transformation had much more to do with something very different, something that was given little time in my friend's transformation group.

A Key to Transformation: The Class Meeting

John Wesley's Kingswood group (which we will talk about in chapter eight) that was gathering in the hive of scum and villainy[4] began to grow to the point that they could no longer meet in homes and public spaces, and needed to build a chapel. In order to do that, everyone involved committed to pay a tiny amount every week, but collecting the offering became problematic for the growing group. They eventually broke themselves down into classes of twelve with one person acting as the leader who went from house to house to collect the offering each week.

This simple act of trying to collect money turned into the most transformative part of John Wesley's ministry. It turned out that when the class leaders checked in during the week to collect the offering, they found that many of the people who were part of the group were not nearly as holy as they said they were when they were meeting together. The leaders uncovered addiction, abuse, and many other issues among the flock. As they had grown, the anonymity of a large group had allowed people to be *more* anonymous and able to hide their shortcomings so that they did not have to do the hard work of surrender.

These classes (of both Christians and non-Christians who were attending the service) began to meet together once a week with the express purpose of helping people make their actions match their beliefs. Their purpose was far from completing a curriculum or going over study sheets completed at home. They focused on watching over each other in love and holding each other mutually accountable.

I know your next question (as long as it is the same as my next question): Accountable to what? Anyone was admitted to the groups who wanted to seriously consider Christianity and begin to attempt to live more righteous lives. They did not have to label themselves "Christian" or be holy people already, just interested in turning in that direction. Then, each week they would seek to help each other live lives that were focused on Wesley's three simple rules:

> First, by doing no harm, by avoiding evil in every kind; especially that which is most gener- ally practiced. Second, by doing good, by being in every kind merciful after their power; as they have opportunity, doing good of every possible sort, and as far as is possible to all men. . . . Thirdly, by attending upon all the ordinances of God. Such are the public worship of God; the ministry of the word, either read or expounded, the Supper of the Lord; private prayer, searching the Scriptures; and fasting, or abstinence.[5]

Doing no harm, doing good, and attending to the ordi- nances of God. Each week they would gather, and the leader would begin by telling about his or her actions in these areas and would ask each person the question: How is it with your soul? By which they would mean, "How are you doing at making your actions reflect the three rules?"

They would talk about their lives, review the places that they had made goals the week before, and talk about what they needed to add, change, or avoid this week. Simple and powerful.

not really non like you talk about your experience of God

These groups were spread throughout the movement Wesley had begun and effected real life change all over England. Wesley even tried changing the focus from these groups later on, only to reinstate them after finding that "Almost all the seed has fallen by the wayside; there is scarce any fruit of it remaining."[6]

Glimpses of Class Meetings in the Scripture

The problem with talking about Scripture in relation to class meetings is that this value did not develop out of some deep pondering of Scripture, but out of a practical ministry adaptation and accidental innovation. That being said, the value of small-group interaction and intimate community is throughout the Scriptures and obviously informed the practice once discovered.

The most powerful small group in the Scriptures is the disciples. The thirteen disciples (twelve without Judas's replacement) are a great test case for the class meeting. When Jesus calls them, they come from all walks of life. From tax collectors to fisherman, the group is incredibly diverse. Though they are diverse, they are treated as peers. By virtue of them being a disciple of Jesus, all of their earthly status is stripped away and they are on a level playing field.

This idea of spiritual equality is spoken about in several places like Colossians 3:11: "Here there is no Gentile or Jew, circumcised or uncircumcised, barbarian, Scythian, slave or free, but Christ is all, and is in all." A life surrendered to Jesus places us all into one category like it did the disciples. They left behind their status to follow Jesus together as one group.

Another interesting thing you see in the life of the disciples is how Jesus led them. They did not camp out in some corner of the temple and open up to page 435 in their disciple manual to discuss the previous week's homework. In fact, the types of settings we see the disciples in are so diverse and so many that it would be useless to try and list them all here. What we get from looking at this example is a clear understanding that teaching in a traditional sense takes a back seat to the myriad of other ways Jesus led the group.

When he did teach them, it went beyond some rote memorization of facts to how they were to live their lives and do ministry. For example, when he taught them about prayer he often turned to the practical, saying things like, "But when you pray, go into your room, close the door . . ." (Matt. 6:6a), or "He said to them, 'When you pray, say . . .'" (Luke 11:2).

Over and over again, Jesus gave them instructions on how they were to live. When they messed up, he corrected them, and he did not ignore an issue so that there would not be conflict. I believe that is because we all need help, and not just help discovering the biblical principles. We need help in very practical ways. We need people who can help us see what the godly reaction is to an overbearing boss, or how we should pray or what we should do with our tax return.

That is what Jesus did for the disciples. He spent the best, most famous, most documented three years of his life guiding them step-by-step so that when he left they might have a clue what he meant when he told them to "go and make disciples of all nations, baptizing them in the name of the Father and of the Son and of the Holy Spirit, and teaching them to obey everything I have commanded you" (Matt. 28:19–20b).

Class-Meeting Moment

I taught my first Bible study when I was in the eighth grade. It sounds absolutely ridiculous, but my youth pastor knew I had felt a call into ministry and equipped me to get some of my friends together to meet and try to grow closer to God. I will never forget the excitement I felt as I prepared for my first meeting. I had a book that was going to give us something spiritual to talk about, I had called everyone to remind them including the mom who was letting us invade her living room, and had even found out that you could get day-old doughnuts at the grocery store for one dollar per dozen. That's right, there were going to be doughnuts at this small group!

We got there, hung out for a little bit, and I made an awkward transition into the spiritual time. We went through the book for a while and then the real powerful moment happened. We asked what people wanted to pray about and the floodgates opened. Some were having big faith questions, some were having a hard time living as Christians at school, and others had horrible relationships with their families.

I had no idea what to do, so we talked about it. What did the other people do when they were in these situations? Who should we ask to get answers to the things we didn't know? And, because the Holy Spirit reveals truth to eighth-graders the same way he does adults, we figured we should end each of these discussions with a commitment to actually *do* something.

Wow. I was overwhelmed at what had happened. I practically floated home and couldn't wait until next week, but nothing would prepare me for what happened the second week. I showed up fifteen minutes early with doughnuts and my roll from the previous week, and was greeted by the guy whose house it was and a friend of his he had invited. Actually, most everyone had invited a friend, and these friends weren't just from our church, some of them didn't even attend church at all.

Week after week we met, spending less and less time on the book, and focusing instead on what was producing real changes in our lives: working on our problems and praying for each other. It turns out that there is a naturalness about this style of small group that organically develops when people are wanting to explore faith and grow closer to God. It turns out that Wesley was onto something.

Class-Meeting Ministry

I know what you are saying, "Wait, didn't you just encourage me to make Bible study and teaching the center of my Sunday school?" Yes. The Sunday school I was talking about was geared at offering a form of the means of sanctifying grace that was the searching of Scriptures. The Bible can be overwhelming to teenagers (and adults) just based on its size. They not only need help in understanding it, but help understanding *how* to understand it. While it may not be necessary for a well-grounded adult Christian to be in a weekly Bible study, it is most likely the best thing for youth to be learning both the what and the how of "searching the Scriptures" in the Sunday school setting.

Class meetings are a different animal. Where the target of the Sunday school groups we talked about in chapter three were primarily committed Christians, these class meetings are meant to include not only Christians, but non-Christians who really want to explore what it means to follow Jesus. Since the groups are concerned with living righteously, it is a great place for seekers to come and get to see the real, struggling faith of Christians.

The first Wesleyan class meetings had twelve members. (I mean, if you have to choose an arbitrary number, you might as well choose one with some biblical significance.) The beautiful thing about that number is that current consensus is that around twelve is just right to be a support-style group. It is the perfect number to have enough people to share the care for a hurting group member where the care does not become a burden. It is a great number for solid conversation, and it is just right to provide for everyone to be relatively well known without having to feel like they must reveal the deepest part of their souls or constantly have something to say.

That is why this size is uniquely suited for the class meeting because the things that a group of about twelve excels at are the same things that are the core values of class meetings. However, there is one stalwart of small groups that is conspicuously missing from that list: curriculum. That is because these groups are not learning-focused groups. They do not have a goal to cover some specific amount of information, and their success is not judged on how much people have learned.

Kevin Watson, in his book about class meetings, calls these types of groups transformation-driven groups. Rather than focusing on discussion or mastery of some subject matter, these groups focus on changed lives.

I don't know what it is about our psyche, but when there is a curriculum, most people feel like they have to finish that week's lesson or they have not done their job. No matter how productive the discussion is, someone will cut it short, pointing out that you haven't even come close to finishing and there's now only ten minutes left. That's why in a class meeting–style group curriculum is kept at an absolute minimum or preferably absent altogether.

So what do you do? How do you set it up? Watson's book, *The Class Meeting*, is a good place to start for people who want to really dive into the model, but the groups are pretty simple. The first step is to recruit your leaders and give them some training time. Since many of them have never been in a group like this, it may be best to start by placing your leaders in a class meeting for a month or two until they get their bearings in this new curriculum-free world. They would be the perfect group to use the Watson book with, as it is designed to teach about class meetings while starting a class meeting group.

After you have your group of trained leaders, it is time to construct the groups. You begin by dividing all the students who are regularly attending into groups with as similar ages as possible. After that is done, you need to do a little bit of teaching with those students about what the group is trying to accomplish and why it has no curriculum.

Then you start the groups. I find that after some hang-out/catch-up time, it is good for the leader to open with prayer and then dive in. I like Wesley's classic three simple rules because they give a simple structure to the conversations. Whatever you use, the point is to get the leader to ask the questions. How have you done this week at fleeing from evil? What about doing good? How is your relationship with God? Have you spent time in prayer, worship, etc.?

The goal of the group is not just sharing, but transformation. Therefore, after the questions are asked, the next step is to decide on a "next step."

The "next step" in each of these areas needs to be small and accomplishable in the next week. A big part of the job of the leader will be helping students set realistic goals. Then, the group leader should write down the goals so they can follow up next week. The group ends by closing in prayer.

It's not rocket science. It turns out that talking about whether or not you are following Jesus and making plans to do better is way more powerful than the well-marketed curriculum you just bought.

Class-Meeting Ministers

This is where the rubber meets the road. American culture has become less and less personal. Though tools like Facebook and Twitter have allowed us to get better at superficial connections (what sociologists call "weak ties"), they have begun to convince us that what we experience there is real relationship.

Don't get me wrong, I think social networks are great, and are fantastic ways to connect with people, but they are not the same thing as sitting in the room with someone or hanging out on the front porch talking about life. They add a layer of anonymity and disconnection, or put another way, they are more impersonal.

That can be dangerous when we talk about life transformation because transformation requires real, vulnerable relationship. As we have less and less of that kind of interaction, we become more and more uncomfortable with it. That discomfort with full-on relationship bleeds into lots of areas, including how we do small groups.

What happens is that in order to deal with our or other people's discomfort with relationship, we choose to make our small groups about something other than life transformation: curriculum. When we do that, we have lost the battle.

But this value is about much more than curriculum. For the pastor this means a commitment to forming real relationships. Facebook it up, tweet every sandwich you ever eat, as long as those are the ways you open the door to real relationships that uncover the soul and seek the piercing, healing light of Christ.

The curriculum issue is a warning that goes far beyond the structure of our small-group ministry. It is a pattern that we have the tendency to repeat over and over again. Faced with the discomfort of walking into a high school lunchroom or hanging out at a football game or listening to someone pour their secrets out on the couch in your office, you choose the good over the great. You spend one more hour preparing your lesson, another fifteen minutes tweaking the logo, and another hour finding just the right set of songs to mirror every aspect of the talk you just spent three hours preparing.

Those parts of our job are important and can make an impact, but nowhere near the impact of a face-to-face conversation about the same information but focused on how that person can live it out in their own life.

→ **Personal Processing**

1. Take a moment to think about each of your last five ministry workdays. How were they spent? Make sure you put an estimated amount of time next to each one.

2. Look at that list. What do you care about the least and can be fully delegated?

3. Now look at the time estimates you wrote down. Where are you spending most of your time? How much of that time could be reallocated, without degrading the quality of your work, in order to carve out more relational time?

4. What is your next step in building more face-to-face ministry opportunities into your week?

➡ **Ministry/Team Processing**

1. Take a moment to list all of the smaller groups that you have at your church or you meet with elsewhere.

2. Go through that list, marking the ones that are heavily curriculum-based as well as the ones that are going well.

3. Make a list of which of those you will transition into class meetings, which ones need to sunset, or which need to be started from scratch.

4. Do you have any leaders that have experience in these sorts of non-curriculum-based groups? What other leaders do you want/need to bring in? How will you train them?

5. How will you divide your students? When will you do some teaching about how these work? When will you launch?

6. Take a moment to discuss with your team how the personal processing challenged you. What is one thing you want to change or do differently as a result?

6

Keepin' It Real

(Bands without Music)

The crowd was buzzing when I arrived at the early morning prayer group I led at my high school. Everyone was talking, and they were all surrounding a guy named Gabe that had only come once the day before. Before I put my backpack down, a girl named Elizabeth ran up to me and blurted, "Have you heard? There's a revival happening in our city!"

I knew enough to understand that Elizabeth was not talking about revivals of the prescheduled variety that happened occasionally throughout the year at most of the churches in town. This was the supernatural act of the Spirit that many of the kids in our group prayed for with fervor every day of the week.

As I walked closer, Gabe's voice cut through the murmurs of the group and I heard him say, "Yeah, every night. The altars have been packed and the people have been falling out all over the place. Last night, we didn't end until two o'clock in the morning!"

I was excited. "Can we go?"

"Totally, we can ride together."

That was it, all plans were canceled for that evening, and I was ready for revival. When we arrived at the church, we took our places and the evangelist spoke about something that I don't recall because no matter what he said it was going to be overshadowed by the wild works of the Spirit that were about to happen. I was sitting next to Gabe when the altar call happened and everyone went down to the altar.

As the evangelist passed and laid hands on each person, they appeared to be passing out like in one of those healing services on TV. I watched everyone fall. After a while they were all up and walking around ready for another dose. That's when I watched as Gabe began to do the same thing. As he prayed for people, they fell out too, and I was impressed.

Later that night, Gabe gathered us in a corner of the room and began to give us the deep thoughts of a high school guru. "This power is cool, isn't it?" We all nodded in assent. "But it's just the Spirit. He's everywhere, and if you open yourself up to him, you can receive the same thing in your room. I fall out all the time in my prayer time at home. Last night, the Spirit told me that being a Christian is about surrendering to the Spirit and that doesn't require anyone else. All you need is you and God. If you don't like your church, you don't need it! All you need is the Word and the Spirit and a place to pray."

I was so on board with this. I didn't need anyone else. I was like MacGyver and all I needed was my room and a Bible, and maybe a CD of the special music they used during the altar times that they sold in the lobby on the way out.

On the way home that night I was dazed and dazzled with the whole experience. I passed on the cigarette that Gabe offered as I closed the passenger door, and tried to figure out how I would get more quiet time away from my family and friends at my house.

• • •

Isolationist Theology

As odd as it sounds to me today, this theology fit my American teen narcissism perfectly. But the more I was around Gabe, the more I saw the horror of a faith lived in isolation. He was morally bankrupt. He denied himself no pleasure, yet had a way to explain it all theologically, resorting to the fact that the "Holy Spirit had told him" it was what he needed to do. Even if you disagreed, there was no response. How do you argue against divine inspiration except to say that it wasn't God talking? And that didn't fly with Gabe.

Putting our thoughts in the mouth of God is incredibly dangerous. Maybe God did tell you something while you were listening or sleeping, but what if that wasn't God? What if it was your overactive imagination or the result of the double-cheese chimichanga you were eating before bed? There's nothing wrong with having a sense of God speaking to us, but when we offer those words to others, it is best to be guarded about the divine inspiration. If it is from God, it will prove true even if scrutinized, and if it turns out that it was something other than God, people will be able to easily let go of its false teaching.

An even bigger problem than Gabe's claim to divine inspiration was the theology he was teaching. It is, of course, totally foreign to how we are instructed to live in the Scriptures. There is no talk of isolation, no words of self-reliance. Rather, we are reminded over and over of our dependence on God and the gift of the community of believers. Neither of those is stated as optional.

Taking Faith to the Next Level: Bands

In this book we have spent some time talking about one of the small community pieces of Wesley's ministry when we talked about the class meeting. But that is far from the end of Wesley's ministry innovation. In addition to that small discipleship-focused group, Wesley developed a model that sought to take those who longed to go deeper to the next level. That group was called the "band," and differed from the class meeting in several significant ways.

If you remember, the class meeting was a mixed grouping of people of varying levels of engagement with faith, all of whom were interested in seeking more. Because of that, many people experienced salvation in those groups and began to try and live according with the directives of Scripture.

The problem is that if the class meeting is the only small-group discipleship option, members can get frustrated constantly trying to meet the needs of people who are at the most basic level of faith. Bands started by requiring that members of a band had already experienced salvation and were on their way in living the Christian life. These groups were concerned with one thing: the serious pursuit of holiness.

The class meeting was the fundamental unit of the movement Wesley began. In fact, they were required for all members. Though you could not be a part of one of Wesley's groups without being involved in a class meeting, bands were totally voluntary and open for any who had been forgiven of their sins and were pursuing holiness.

The key difference in the two groups was their approach to the pursuit of holiness. The class meeting approached the basic level of actions. When members discussed, they were focused on understanding the commands of Scripture and how they were to be lived out. The bands, on the other hand, would focus on the heart and motivations.[7] It was their goal to deal with surrendering the heart fully to the power of the love of the Holy Spirit. The focus was on the internal rather than the external.

Their fundamental difference in focus was echoed in differences in structure as well. Since all of these people were further along the spiritual path, they did not require a leader. Instead, they shared those responsibilities, focusing on mutual accountability and caring for each other.

One of the things that Wesley recognized was that if one was to bare the most hidden parts of their soul to others, the groups needed to be made up of members in as similar life situations as possible. That meant that the days of mixed age/gender groups were gone. These were as specific as they could be in making sure members were truly peers. There were single women societies, ones for married women and married men, as well as young men and women.

Every week when they met they would open with a prayer or song and then give an account of any sins they committed in thought, word, or action, and any temptations they had felt. They would talk about how they had been forgiven and repented of those sins, and then would talk through the places where they were unsure whether or not an act was a sin. They were meticulous in their quest for entire sanctification and sought the support of their brothers and sisters in Christ.

To help them on this quest Wesley wrote the "Rules of the Band Societies." Beyond giving them specific directions for how the meeting was to run and the questions they were to ask each week, he instructed them as to the things that were expected of them in life. They were to carefully abstain from doing evil, paying special attention to the Sabbath, honesty in business, frugality in their finances, modesty in their dress, and avoid using alcohol or tobacco. They were to zealously do good works, paying special attention to giving to the poor, and reproving those who sin. Finally, they were to focus on the ordinances of God, specifically on church attendance, private prayer, filling every vacant hour with the study of the Scriptures, and observing a fast on every Friday.[8]

Glimpses of Bands in the Scriptures

Though Wesley developed his bands long after the completion of the writing of the biblical canon, the Scripture's focus on relational discipleship runs deep. Gabe might have been disappointed to learn that the Lone Ranger approach to spirituality is not really what Jesus was going for. He was clear over and over again that partnership in both ministry as well as one's personal discipleship was key.

At the center of the whole idea is the way in which Jesus discipled the disciples—as a group. He did not merely find an apprentice and mentor them; he gathered a band of disciples and lived with them for years, sharing the most intimate and normal moments with them. When he was ready to send out people to expand his earthly ministry in Luke 10, Jesus did not commission them and send out seventy-two individuals to seventy-two different locations. He sent them out in pairs. He sent them out with partners in discipleship. This commitment to relational discipleship was so deep that when faced with the task of telling the entire world about Jesus, the disciples and apostles still didn't abandon this relational approach. Over and over again in Scripture, you find verses like Acts 12:25, "When Barnabas and Saul had finished their mission, they returned from Jerusalem, taking with them John, also called Mark." Christianity is not a solo endeavor.

The Scripture that speaks closest to what happened in the band meetings comes from James 5:16: "Therefore confess your sins to each other and pray for each other so that you may be healed. The prayer of a righteous person is powerful and effective." Confession is a powerful thing. Not only does it break the stranglehold of secrecy, it allows another to come alongside us in our path toward holiness.

That sense of having someone "come alongside" us is another aspect of the bands that can be seen in the Scriptures from Galatians 6:2: "Carry each other's burdens, and in this way you will fulfill the law of Christ." This verse comes immediately after a verse talking about being tempted and implies that it is our job as partners in discipleship to not merely help people turn back to Jesus and ask forgiveness, but to help discover the roots of the temptation itself and work with them to remove the roots of temptation as well as the flowers of sin it produces.

All of this is built on the Old Testament concept of confession. Over and over again, they were called to go to the priest and confess their sin, bring an offering, and allow the priest to offer it in their place for the sin they committed. It was both a means for forgiveness and opportunity for discipleship. It is why it is important to incorporate these values in our own lives and ministries.

Band Moment

I started my first youth band (we call them "Life Groups") at a moment when I saw kids who were enjoying our standard ministries but feeling frustrated by their lack of depth. I knew that if we changed the ministries to meet the needs of those few students, we would alienate the rest.

My first response was to offer an in-depth Bible study. I figured that's what they meant by "deep" when I asked them about our group. However, I soon found out that these students were very capable of studying the Bible on their own and were. Though some of them appreciated some higher-level teaching, many of them never came more than once or twice.

Frustrated yet again, I decided to try something from my Wesleyan history class: the band. At our next youth meeting I made a simple announcement, "If you are wanting to go deep in a relationship with God and partner with friends to help you grow closer to God, these groups are for you. If you are interested, get a couple of friends and let us know so that we can connect you with an adult leader."

I had no idea what to expect from our first meeting. We made surface conversation for five minutes and after opening with prayer I said, "This group is about helping you, but we can't do that without knowing where you struggle. Let's go around and share the top struggles as we get started."

To my complete astonishment, they were completely honest. The first guy talked about his struggle with pornography and how he felt trapped in a destructive habit. Most of the other guys chimed in that they were struggling with that too or had in the past. The next guy talked about his temptation with his girlfriend and the mistakes they were making most weekends. The next guy talked about sneaking alcohol from his dad at home. The next revealed his struggle with rage. Keep in mind, these were the "top kids" who everyone else believed were as close to God as a teen could be. They were the ones asked to pray at school clubs and lead music for the mission team.

But we didn't leave it there. We talked about surrender. We talked about the power of the Spirit, and we talked about how we could support each other in surrendering. The relationships that were formed in that group still hold those young men up in difficult times.

Band Ministry

The bands remind us that the key to living a life of obedience is deep, accountable relationships that spur us on to more. The problem is that our ministries can tend to focus on the surface.

Why is that? If you have read just about any book published about ministry in the past twenty years, you will have seen some version of what I call the commitment cone. Starting at the largest end, there is your community or local context, and then in graduated levels from there into the cone are labels for groups of people who are increasingly committed and increasingly smaller. Though, at times, this diagram can seem to be stating the obvious, it makes sense that there are less super-committed people than surface-level people. This is a fact of life in any organization.

In ministries, our goal is to encourage and equip people to move into those deeper levels in their commitment to faith. The problem is that we can get distracted from that mission by planning for the larger groups of less-committed people. It's nice to be able to report big numbers from an event at a church meeting, but those events take a lot of time and resources to plan. The large

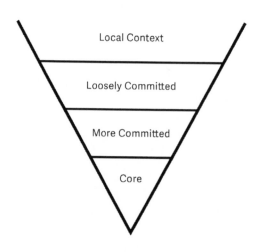

number of kids requires more volunteers to supervise them and even more pizza to feed them.

Don't get me wrong, big events are part of a healthy ministry, but those big events can become a distraction from what really matters. And the reason they become a distraction is because the large numbers make it easy to feel like (and calculate) they have a larger impact than other ministries. The problem is that the real discipleship is playing a trick on our brains. The real, deep transformation happens at those deeper levels with fewer kids.

Situated at that deepest level with the least number of students is the band ministry. Aside from an obvious need to change the name of this type of ministry, there are several tweaks that make sense for bringing the values of the bands into a twenty-first-century ministry for teens.

The homogeneity of the groups is important. Students need to feel like the other students in the room understand what is going on with them. With the plethora of different groups and subgroups of students, it is best to let go of the fiction that anyone besides a teen can understand exactly who all those groups are and how they function. That means that you cannot be the person to decide what type of students you will open up a group for; rather, you can ensure homogeneity by asking those who express an interest to invite some of their own friends and form a group of people they already trust.

However, homogeneity can only go so far with teenage accountability. The reality is that they simply do not have the life experience or knowledge to deal effectively with many of life's situations. I believe that bands with teens need to be set up with a significantly older guide or guides whom the youth leader considers to be wise. Their role is not to teach, but to help students process, answer questions, and guide the students along the narrow path.

The content of the group time needs little alteration. These groups are primarily about experiencing the power and healing of the Spirit, as we are faithful to live out the Bible's call on us to confess our sins to each other. The leader may like to be more informal about the group time, asking how everyone's week was and following up with questions about sin, etc., or it may be better for each group to develop their own rule of life like Wesley did in those early days for his people with the three simple rules. Either way, the goal is an increasing surrender to the Holy Spirit's power to bring about the gift of holiness in our lives.

Band Ministers

You need a band. Period. Though this was a voluntary group for the average people involved in the Methodist movement, Wesley required anyone in leadership to be a part of this important tool for transforming individuals into the likeness of Christ.

Ministry can be taxing not just on our time and energy, but on our souls as well. There are moments in my life as a pastor when I realize that every bit of my time has been used on developing others, and I have neglected my own relationship with God. However, those seasons in which I've had the gift of being a part of a band, there was a constant reminder to not lose focus on my own spiritual life.

I will add one caution to this call to bands. Be careful about being in a band with those you are leading as a pastor. Remember, this group is about surrounding yourself with peers in similar stages of life and feeling free to bare your soul to them. Your role as their pastor is not something you can set aside and means that you will never come into that group as a peer. In addition, there may be times when you need to confess something with the right church council member that could endanger your job. I know this can be hard, but with all the different ways to communicate without being in the same room, you have it a lot easier than the ministers in Wesley's day!

Though this has serious personal implications, it also has a lot to say about how we live as pastors in general. As a matter of fact, it has its source in something that is written deep into our hearts as pastors. I can't tell you the number of times I have heard people complain that some ministry leader or another is "just about the numbers." Part of what is being expressed here is that some people only care about getting crowds of people to show up, and they measure success in ministry by whether or not that is happening.

However, the reason this chafes at the heart of many Christians is that there is something deep within us that knows that the key to making real life change is in these super-small groups of believers that band together to help each other grow closer to God. Every time we have a great meeting with a group of people and are asked "How was the turnout?" we recoil because we know that the reality might be that the opposite of what the questioner is looking for (smaller attendance) is likely to produce more lasting life change in the people who showed up.

Watch out if you have an event that does surprisingly well attendance-wise. The ego-stroking that you will receive as a result is likely to have you permanently seeking a repeat of that giant attendance. I have watched as friends have run their families, personal health, and emotional well-being into the ground trying to top themselves over and over again, each time putting in more hours and doing more over-the-top antics. All of that so that they could say, "We had more there than last year," or even better, "We had more at this retreat than we ever have."

Bands call us to leave the crowd of people and gather three or four and do the hard work of surrendering to the love of the Holy Spirit day after day. This means that we put a priority on these meetings in the same way we do the giant back-to-school scavenger hunt or the annual bonfire. We carve out time, and don't allow the demands of the crowd to allow us to put it off. We model this for our students and volunteers and praise them for putting the needs of their few above the lure of the crowd.

→ **Personal Processing**

1. If you do not have a band, what three or four fellow Christians, who do not go to your church, would you be willing to embark on this band-style journey with?

2. Open your calendar and set a deadline for contacting them to set up the first meeting.

3. Take a moment to think about each of the last five ministry workdays you have spent. What percentage of your time was spent on crowd-oriented ministries as opposed to class-meeting and band-style ministries?

4. What do you think would be the appropriate percentage? What do you need to do to make your schedule match your priorities?

→ Ministry/Team Processing

1. Take a moment to consider your small-group gatherings. Do any of them fit Wesley's band model? Are any of them close?

2. What would need to be changed to push some of the existing groups toward Wesley's band model? Would that be a good idea?

3. It all starts with leaders. Which of your leaders would you trust to lead these sorts of groups? What additional training would they need to start?

4. How would you advertise this group to your students in a way that didn't take away from their class-meeting-style group but open up this voluntary next step to them?

5. How many students do you think you would need to accommodate at the beginning of this offering?

6. Take a moment to discuss with your team how the personal processing challenged you. What is one thing you want to change or do differently as a result?

Part Three

Reclaiming Mission— Bigger Than Me

Let our hearts be joined herein; let us unite our wishes and prayers; let our whole soul pant after a general revival of pure religion and undefiled, the restoration of the image of God, pure love, in every child of man.

—John Wesley

Sermon #132, on Laying the Foundation of the New Chapel, Near the City Road, London

7

Sacred Questioning

(Quadrilateral for Skeptics)

Luke was one of the most intelligent people I had ever met in my sixteen years on this earth. Not only did he read the schoolbooks that I never could manage to figure out how to open, he read other books about philosophy and computer programming.

Luke was a ton of fun to be around. However, when he chose to focus his intellect on faith, his questions could be piercing, and watch out if he was in a skeptical mood!

As Luke and our friends walked into Sunday school, I could see that he had that look in his eye. Somewhere between playful and dangerous, his eyes lit up with skepticism. He had seen the lesson a week before and had come with his questions preloaded. Today was going to be interesting.

The lessons were the typical fare for Sunday school at the time. Some Scripture, some thoughts, some questions, and we're done. This one was talking about the granddaddy of all problems: creation.

We started by reading Genesis 2 and then Genesis 1. The teacher actually mentioned that chapter one was probably written after chapter two, which basically blew my mind from the beginning. Then it came time for questions, and Luke opened up with full force. In five minutes he leveled some of the most difficult questions about God and the Bible.

He began with, "Why does the Bible get the whole story wrong? Why doesn't it match with science?" The teacher made some response that Luke dismissed so quickly that the next question hit like a sucker punch. "What I really want is proof. Where is the proof that God even exists? Where is the data?" This time silence was the response. Luke wasn't fazed. He continued asking how one decided to leave out parts of the Bible. The teacher fell right into that trap saying he believed the whole Bible, at which point Luke went into the dietary laws and asked if the teacher had ever consumed a steak with blood in it.

At that point the teacher tapped out with the statement that too many of us use when we have no idea how to answer questions: "Luke, there are some things you just have to accept on faith."

Luke could recognize when someone couldn't take any more of his relentless questioning and seeking answers, and let several minutes pass in silence as class came to a close.

• • •

Silenced Questions

The most tragic part of this story is its ending. This incredibly intelligent young believer ended up feeling that Christianity was not credible enough to stand up to his questions. For him it seemed weak, and he ended up spending many years as an atheist.

Part of the reason for his abandonment of the faith is that when faced with difficult questions, the volunteer Sunday school leader missed an opportunity and maybe didn't even see the opportunity for what it was. Often times when people come with a question, their initial question is just the beginning. Students like Luke will use a question like that to crack open the door to their boundless curiosity to see if they are in a safe place for them to explore and discover.

In Luke's case, his playfulness with questions was a sign of his engaging the fullness of his considerable intellect with his faith. It was great! It was something to be praised and developed, but instead it was minimized and silenced.

This volunteer was probably not trying to silence or minimize Luke, but his response betrays a deep cultural problem in many churches: we are afraid of questions. The fear is based in many camps. For some, they do not want people on the fence to be knocked off by someone's difficult statements. For others, their fear comes from a personal theology that is built on the shaky ground of quick answers and ignored doubts. Still others see engaging seriously with questions as a sign of unfaithfulness. Though all of these positions are sincere, they ignore the fact that intellectual engagement with theology through questioning is a primary way in which most people grow and strengthen their foundation.

Quadrilateral: The Four-Fold Solution

For those who are involved in the theological tradition begun by Wesley, we have a great method for dealing with this difficult area: the quadrilateral. This method for investigating theological questions was not something that John Wesley put together himself, but was birthed out of a thoughtful reflection on Wesley's life and works. A brilliant scholar named Albert Outler was the first to bring this pattern to the forefront. After spending hours upon hours poring over Wesley's life and writings, he came to notice a pattern in the way that Wesley processed his own theological conundrums. After much refinement, he submitted this system to the world as the innate pattern within Wesley that gave rise to his life and theology.

What Outler discovered was that John Wesley processed belief in a multifaceted way—incorporating several sources of authority, weighing them against each other, and building a cohesive perspective from their insight.

The model begins with Scripture. This was the beginning of everything for Wesley. If you have ever read any of his sermons, it can be difficult to see the points at which Wesley gives his own insights because so much of what he says is a quotation or close paraphrase of the Scripture. That is because, for Wesley, Scripture was the thing that held all of life and belief together. It was the clearest source of God's revealed knowledge to humanity, and the foundation upon which all other beliefs were built.

In this model, one must be constantly engaging with the Scripture. At every point in the questioning process, we return to this anchor and see how its light changes the perspective we are gaining from other sources. In other words, <u>Scripture not only is the beginning of knowledge</u>, <u>but holds all other forms of knowledge accountable</u>.

However, Scripture is not always clear or as detailed as we need it to be. It turns out that not only are the Scriptures written in ancient languages, but are also highly cultural. All the instructions were written to specific people in specific places at specific times within specific cultures. Likewise, the stories are those that captivated and enlightened the minds of people thousands of years ago—the stories drew on images from their world and referenced the artifacts of imagination within their time.

All that means is that not only may Scripture not speak specifically to a single issue, but its words may be so bound to the original context that the truth behind them is drastically different than it may appear at first blush. Luckily, we do not live in a vacuum. We have a host of other sources of authority to help us consider and discern theological truths.

The first of those is tradition. Wesley was firmly rooted in the Anglican tradition of his day, going so far as to forbid the formation of a separate Methodist church until after he passed. However, tradition is far more than your choice of historical theological system.

Tradition in this setting should be thought of in terms of the connection to the thoughts and life examples of all those that have gone before us, both living and dead. When we call our grandmother and ask for her advice, we are consulting a source of tradition. When we read the biography of one of the great saints of old like Teresa of Avila, we are consulting a source of tradition. And when we look at the statements of belief decided upon by church councils and conferences, we are consulting a source of tradition. When all of these sources are used to help fill out the principles found in the Scriptures, we begin to have a sense of rootedness and confidence that those whom we respect, who have gone before, are lending their voice to the theological dialogue we are using to develop our understanding of God.

However, the reality is that all of that can become a bit much. In fact, volumes upon volumes have been composed in theological battles between the very people we will consult in regard to tradition. Even when held accountable by Scripture, we can end up with more than a few divergent views on any given theological topic.

That is where the next source of authority comes in: reason. I know, it may seem ridiculous to actually engage your logical mind and apply reason to a debate on theology, but bear with me here. All of this has to be looked at critically to work. For Wesley, reason was key. Though he did not believe that it could, on its own, create the sort of living faith that we are called to as Christians, he believed that when one applied their reasonable mind to understanding any issue at hand, reason could make the leap of faith in those findings easier.

Reason is especially important as we interact with the world of science. If data is the king of science, reason is its queen. When the church refuses to accept well-reasoned science, and instead chooses to challenge that intelligently interpreted data with the implications of ancient poetry, we fall flat. Rather, we should use those well-reasoned conclusions about the way God's creation works and is put together to help understand and explain God.

Still, the most well-reasoned arguments can be proved false. Over and over again science has revealed that no matter how "obvious" something may be to our logical mind, if it doesn't work in practice, it must be rejected for a more accurate model.

That is the role of the final piece of our model for asking faith questions: experience. Experience is tricky because to some it sounds like, "Do whatever you want, it's no big deal." It couldn't be further from that. Experience is much more like a validity test. It is not saying to try it out and see what you think, but it is experience in the terms of hindsight is twenty-twenty. After beginning with Scripture, consulting the sources of tradition, and using reason to bring it all together, does your concept match with your experience of the world? With the understanding that the Holy Spirit lives within us and is our guide to all truth (see John 16:13), this consultation of our own heart and life is a consultation with the Holy Spirit. Put in spiritual terms, consulting experience is seeking the witness of the Holy Spirit within us.

This piece takes the questioning out of the realm of the theoretical and forces us to realize that all theology is meant to be lived out in our lives as we surrender to the Holy Spirit. If the way we understand God does not influence and inform our life in the world, we have not completed the process and our understanding is flawed. Experience asks the questions, "Does this *actually* work in the world? Does it match with what the Holy Spirit has shown me?" From there, the quest is to take the understanding and allow it to find expression in your day-to-day life and actions.

This system of seeking to understand who God is and who we are is a single system with each piece being interwoven and dependent on the rest. When we are able to bring all of those sources of authority into focus on a single issue, we can be confident in our understanding. Methodists have historically had a great way of expressing this as a single, whole, system. They say, "Wesley believed that the living core of the Christian faith was revealed in Scripture, illumined by tradition, vivified in personal experience, and confirmed by reason. Scripture is primary, revealing the Word of God 'so far as it is necessary for our salvation.'"[9] That is it; all those pieces of authority working together provide a path to understanding.

Glimpses of the Quadrilateral in Scripture

Though this is a system culled from the life of a follower of Jesus, there are clear roots in the Scripture that extend the understanding of all the pieces of the system.

Beginning with Scripture, there are many verses that allow us to see both its primacy in matters of belief as well as its basis of authority. In 2 Timothy, Paul addresses both of those issues in 3:16–17, saying "All Scripture is God-breathed and is useful for teaching, rebuking, correcting and training in righteousness, so that the servant of God may be thoroughly equipped for every good work." The beauty of this verse is in its simple clarity. No matter who the vessel was for the particular Scripture, we believe that it all came from the deepest parts of God, and it was he who breathed it into existence through the minds and hearts of the writers.

However, God was not some author writing for the fun of it in his basement, all Scripture was given with a purpose; namely, to instruct our lives of faith. That role of instruction is clear in the verse from 2 Timothy, and is brought to life in Psalm 119:105, "Your word is a lamp for my feet, a light on my path." Like a lamp in the woods on a dark night, God's Word exposes the edges of thorns and thistles. It reveals immorality for what it is and helps the believer discern the path to life.

The statement that brings the most clarity to this discussion comes as the conclusion to the Sermon on the Mount. After giving his thoughts on everything from adultery to murder to holier-than-thou religious people, Jesus says that those who follow his word build their life on a firm foundation. Which is why setting Scripture as foundational in matters of belief is absolutely essential. If we believe what it says about itself, that it is the Word of God, then the words of Jesus extend beyond his single sermon to cover the entirety of the Bible.

Tradition in the quadrilateral has an incredible metaphoric explanation in Hebrews 12:1, "Therefore, since we are surrounded by such a great cloud of witnesses, let us throw off everything that hinders and the sin that so easily entangles. And let us run with perseverance the race marked out for us." This comes after a recitation of the work of God in the lives of the early fathers of Judaism. It reminds us that it is not just a written text that reveals God to us, but the lives of those who have gone before us. It is their example in words and deeds that continues to shine the light of Christ in our lives.

Reason pops up in a diversity of forms in the Scriptures. In 1 Peter, we are instructed to "Always be prepared to give an answer to everyone who asks you to give the reason for the hope that you have" (3:15). This indicates the use of our own abilities of reason to draw from disparate sources to construct viable answers. On the other side of that same coin, Paul appeals to the people's reason when instructing them about idols. He says, "I speak to sensible people; judge for yourselves what I say" (1 Cor. 10:15). Beyond all that, we have examples of reason being applied by the great host of witnesses in the Bible to make sense of life and belief.

Experience is seen throughout the Scripture as the imperative to take what one knows and then continue the discernment by living it out in one's life. One of the things I love about the parable of the Good Samaritan is the way in which it puts on display the idea of Scripture, tradition, and reason being vivified by experience. At the outset of the parable, we discover that an expert in the law is giving this as a response to a law question. He asks, "What must I do to inherit eternal life?" (Luke 10:25b). This was an incredibly divisive issue at the time and one that merited many words (and in turn references to Scripture, tradition, and reason). Jesus skipped the detailed argument for a story of a man living and showing mercy. After this beautiful story (which most likely exposed the hypocrisy of the one asking the original question), Jesus' final answer to this technical question is to tell the expert in the law to "go and do likewise" (Luke 10:37b). He answers with experience in the hopes that the man would complete his knowledge by living it out in his life.

Separating them out and finding the passages that are scattered throughout the Scriptures is useful, but only as long as we bring it all back together. If you remember, this system flowed from the life of John Wesley; it wasn't developed in some sort of academic vacuum, but in the mess of life. That is where it belongs: in the mess of life being used to help gather thoughts and concepts into a useful framework for following Jesus.

Quadrilateral Moment

"My thoughts are everywhere." J. R. was one of the most intelligent and perceptive students in our group, and was sitting on the comfy chair in my office used by students when they needed to have a serious discussion.

J. R. had a list of questions that would make even a seasoned professor flinch. Over the years his considerable intellect had discovered just about every big question we face as Christians, and he was unloading them in my office.

If there's one thing I've learned about helping teens navigate the path from inherited beliefs to self-owned beliefs it is that giving them my personal take ends up hurting more than it does helping. So, with each question I responded with my standard, "Well, tell me what is bothering you about it."

Then, he would confess, "I just don't know how a good God can allow such things." Or, "I feel like science and faith don't match," or, "What kinds of proof do we even have that God exists?"

There it was: the opportunity to begin searching the Scriptures together. That's where we began. We took one at a time over several weeks and explored the key passages. From there I would help him learn how to evaluate sources and discover historical approaches and we would agree to do some research and meet to compare notes.

Over the next several months that's what we did until J. R. emerged with fully formed beliefs about these troubling questions. He still wasn't sure exactly what I believed except that I wanted to help him form a belief that was true to the Scripture and made sense in his life. It was truly his belief.

not unspokenly / some I think that / is the best approach

Quadrilateral Ministry

The quadrilateral is meant to color all of our spiritual life. Which means that focusing on a single program or event as the primary way it is expressed in your ministry would not be true to the DNA of the quadrilateral. It must be expressed throughout our ministries, and it begins with a comfort level with questioning that may make some . . . uncomfortable.

There is nothing wrong with questioning; in fact, it is one of the most important paths of growth in teens. Questions mean that they are engaging with their faith. Questions mean that they are actively trying to make sense of God in their world. However, for those who grew up in a different time or culture or feel they have all the answers worked out, questions can feel like denial. When those emotions crop up, questioners can be silenced, shamed, or both in an effort to protect the curious individual as well as the others in the room from their own weak faith. That is the opposite of the response we want to foster. What we want to do is to encourage students who are investigating their questions of faith to look for answers using the quadrilateral.

There are several factors we need to add to our times with students to create this environment. First, and foremost, we praise questions. When students ask questions of us, we say something like, "I love it when students ask me questions!" Then, if we have the answer, we phrase it in a narrative that includes us asking the question like, "When I asked that question I found this Scripture helpful . . ." All of that serves to reinforce that questions are good, and that even the mighty pastor asks them. If you do not know the answer, that is great because you and the student get to discover it together!

When we have those opportunities, those gifts, to answer the question of a student, it is an opportunity to teach the method behind the answer, not just the answer. Therefore, when we respond, we make sure to utilize the pattern of the quadrilateral in our answer. We begin by talking about the Scripture that addresses whatever question we are considering, and though it may be a simple answer from the Scripture, it is important to talk about what would happen if it wasn't that simple. . . . What if it wasn't so clear? Then we would look at history and our trusted mentors. From there we would work out all those facts reasonably and figure out how they match with our life and how they resonate with the Holy Spirit. Most important, we push our answer to conclude by considering how this information changes how we live in the world.

Recognizing that difficult questions about faith encourage curiosity and faith formation as students are intrigued and encouraged to find answers impacts our choice of curriculum and topics for any up-front teaching. The fact is that classes bearing the term "basic" or "101" communicate to students that no matter how much Sunday school they have been through, we still can't trust them to figure things out on their own. What is better is to find ways to teach the basics of faith as parts of answering the tough questions our students are facing.

Especially with the high value placed on Scripture in this system, it is important to understand concepts like inspiration, infallibility, and the history of the development of the Bible. It is important to understand how it is structured, who wrote it, and why it can be trusted. On their own, those concepts can be dry and downright boring. However, placed within the context of an intriguing question or issue, these dry concepts come to life. For example, there have been many "gospels" discovered in recent history that are not included in the biblical canon (and The History Channel has made a pretty penny on touting their stories). This fact is sensational, and begs the question: Why are they not in the Bible? They are old and talk about Jesus and are written in weird ancient languages—why are they treated differently? The answer is to explore all of those formerly dry concepts to discover what makes them less reliable. What a gift!

The final piece of quadrilateral programming is my personal favorite: the question night. We all have in-between nights right before or after a retreat where it is difficult to plan, or the moments when the person who was scheduled to lead doesn't show. The response is usually some version of a game-night tap dance. Instead of busting out Scattergories next time, try this powerful spontaneous option.

If possible, divide the group into two groups with similar ages and take them in turn. You begin by passing out cards and pencils and give them an open-ended invitation to ask any question they have about the Bible, faith, spirituality, etc. If your group hasn't done much questioning before, you might prime them with some questions you've heard before (or already know the answers to) like: "Where are the dinosaurs?" "How can evolution and the Bible agree?" "What about people who spend their whole life in another country and don't hear about Jesus?" You collect the questions and spend the rest of your time answering as many as you can. You will most likely have some left over that you can spend more time on in upcoming weeks or on a blog.

If you don't trust your ability to answer these, invite your pastor or the resident theology nerd volunteer to tag-team it with you. The key to being successful here is twofold: not giving shallow answers, and making sure you have answers for your own (likely similar) questions.

Quadrilateral Ministers

The reality is that between planning the ultimate mudslide party and counseling teens in crisis, you may have not given yourself time to answer your own questions. The other side of the coin is you may have your own baggage in regard to questioning that was passed down from the church of your childhood. Whatever the case, in order to live fully into this aspect of a Wesleyan faith, you need to both become comfortable questioning and spend some time allowing those questions to spark some research and personal development.

This comfort with and method for exploring questions means something significant for our lives as pastors. We are not people who dogmatically argue theological minutiae. On the other hand, we recognize that anything as significant as faith in a supernatural deity will necessarily be so complex as to cause many questions that do not have quick, easy answers. In fact, anything this complex will likely mean that there will be perspectives that seem to be equally true and totally disagree. Our role as pastors is to nurture people's ability to navigate the gray waters of difficult questions and find places of peace in their understanding.

The unfortunate reality of the church's history of silencing and shaming those who ask significant questions is that many have opted out of faith altogether because the anti-questioning reaction has given the impression that our faith cannot stand up to serious scrutiny. These people who have been pushed to the margins and out the doors need pastors who are comfortable with questions and are able to walk with people through their struggles with faith.

The problem is that they don't often darken the doors of a church. Though they may not attend, they have friends and family who do and want to help them come to a place of faith and reap the rewards of a life lived in obedience to God. Because there are so few pastors who seriously deal with these kinds of questions, you will open yourself up as a unique presence in your community. If you are intentional at mentioning this fact and prove your sincerity by actually doing it, you will find a steady stream of students setting up coffee appointments and aunts giving you e-mail addresses of their nephews. You will break into a new field ripe for the harvest as you become a quadrilateral pastor.

➜ **Personal Processing**

1. Think about your own level of comfort. On a scale of one to four, with one being denial and four being ceaselessly curious, where does your own comfort level with

questions fall? What would you need to do to increase that comfort level?

2. Make a list of your own big questions about faith. Who could you go to lunch with to explore the answers to those questions more fully?

3. What about your students? What questions have you heard from them? If none, ask around your volunteers—what questions have they heard?

4. What is your next step in reaching out to questioning students this week?

➡ Ministry/Team Processing

1. Take a moment to consider your teaching-based ministries. How hospitable are their schedules to identifying and dealing with students' questions?

2. Consider your leaders. How comfortable are they with questions? If there is a general hostility toward questioning, think about a short training around creating a culture of questioning.

3. Along those same lines, what teens in your group are most knowledgeable and open to questioning that could support your own quest to find answers?

4. How about your choices in curriculum and topics? How do they do at capturing the intellectual imagination of your students? How are they at creating curiosity? What are some other curricula or topics that you can adopt?

5. Look at your schedule for the next several months. When would be a good time to schedule a question night as part of an existing ministry?

6. Take a moment to discuss with your team how the personal processing challenged you. What is one thing you want to change or do differently as a result?

8

A New Kind of Mission Work

(The Coal Mines of the Twenty-First Century)

It was getting close to Christmastime, which, if you're not careful, can be a time of immense guilt for Christians as we spend far more money than we have to make sure we give and receive the coolest new everything. One of the churches I attended had a great way to assuage that guilt: Operation Christmas Tree.

The basic idea was that small groups of people picked cards with wish lists from needy families in the neighboring community and purchased the gifts. Not wanting anyone to give something without getting full credit, the classes made sure to wrap all the presents, dress in their nicest Christmas attire, and go deliver the gifts to the whole family on a Sunday afternoon.

The youth group took several cards, did fundraisers (so we didn't have to spend our own Christmas gift money), and bought the presents. On the preordained Sunday, we had a wrapping party, complete with Christmas music and way too much cider and sausage balls, where we wrapped the gifts and piled into cars.

We set out to the area of town where people did not buy new Christmas sweaters each year and drove up to the trailer of the family our car had been assigned. I remember the uncomfortable feeling beginning as we walked up to the house. We knocked on the door and a very surprised-looking father opened it, discovering way more people than he expected holding gifts and beaming with Christmas spirit. He had obviously not been in on the whole Operation Christmas Tree thing and yelled for his wife to come to the door.

When she did, tears filled her eyes and she said thank you in as many ways as any of us had ever heard. She was attracting most everyone's attention, but I couldn't take my eyes off the dad. He was not teary-eyed. I couldn't quite place the emotion (somewhere between angry and ashamed), but it was just about the opposite of what we expected.

What made the whole experience even more weird was that the night before we delivered the gifts, one of my friends that was delivering Christmas cheer to this family with me had told me something truly troubling. His dad had been out of a job for a while and had to tell his family that they couldn't give gifts that Christmas. I kept wondering what would happen if we had showed up on his front step. I wondered if his dad would be the one thanking us through happy tears or standing in the back acting like he wanted us to leave with the gifts we had brought with us.

• • •

Feel-Good Mission

Deep within the layers of problems in this story is our preference to do mission work that makes us feel good. We like to give extravagantly the things that we like to receive ourselves. We enjoy the sort of mission work that allows us to have fun with our friends, "bless" the "poor people," and spend plenty of time patting each other on the back for the difference we are making. Not only that, it is most effective when we can find some place to go (read that as "visit") in order to make an impact. Sure, there are some poor people near us, but there are even poorer people elsewhere.

The problem is that this method does not come close to following the pattern set out by Jesus, and it definitely doesn't follow his teachings on how we are to live and serve our world. When Jesus came into the world, he came as a lower middle class or poor person depending on the commentary you read. He lived with people, developed relationships with them, and met their needs both spiritual and physical. It was messy. He had to deal with irritating people; he had to watch as those he healed did not express gratitude. He had to watch as his closest disciples turned their backs on him. But he did it anyway.

Operation Christmas Tree was the opposite of this. Sure, it was clean and full of upside for those delivering the gifts, but it lacked basic traits that we should look for in good mission work. Not only did the father not know we were coming and was humiliated by his lack of ability to provide what the people in our church thought was an adequate Christmas, but we never saw them again. This was not about forming a relationship with them to help them lift themselves out of poverty. It was about making us feel good at Christmas by giving presents to people who had less than we did.

Drunkards, Criminals, and Revival

I always find theology easiest to understand when I learn it through the life or story of someone I respect. As far as mission is concerned, I believe that John Wesley gives us an incredible example in his ministry to the coal-mining town of Kingswood.

By all accounts, this area of England was godforsaken. The skin covered with coal dust from hours of working in the mines was the cleanest part of them. The people here were so rough that priests would not serve there. They were so rough, and the area so dangerous, that anyone with any morality steered clear. It was so bad that several people taunted a preacher named Whitefield, who felt called to convert heathens, by saying if he wanted to convert heathens, why didn't he go to Kingswood? This was, of course, a ridiculous taunt, as no one with any self-respect would ever go there. No one except Whitefield, who went just a few months later.

What he found was exactly as everyone had heard. It was full of people who were as far from God as anyone had ever seen. These were people who would never consider darkening the door of a church and who would most likely be asked to leave if they did. Instead of finding a nice parish to begin working at and preaching in, Whitefield went to where these people worked (the coal mines) and stood in nearby fields preaching when shifts changed. Thousands came, and Whitefield invited his friend John Wesley to come join him.

After much wrestling, Wesley decided to check it out and had soon moved in and set up shop in the city next to the mines named Bristol.[10] He began organizing small groups and intensive accountability groups. He was constantly preaching to whomever would listen (rarely speaking to less than a thousand at a time) and helping those who chose to turn and follow Jesus to figure out what that meant in a place like Kingswood.

After living there for a while, Wesley and the people he was serving decided to do something to make a difference in the lives of every child in Kingswood. They decided to not let another generation languish in such a desperate situation. They made plans to build a school. They bought the land, laid the cornerstone, and began building.

Not long after all that Wesley wrote in his journal that the area had been transformed. He said, "Kingswood does not now, as a year ago, resound with cursing and blasphemy. It is no longer the seat of drunkenness, uncleanness, and all idle diversions that lead thereto. It is no longer filled with wars and fightings, with clamor and bitterness, with strife and envying. Peace and love are now there."[11]

This was the very beginning of the revolutionary movement that came from Wesley's life and work, and though he traveled extensively over the rest of his long life, he spent more time in Bristol than any other single place.

This is the sort of work Jesus is talking about when he delivers the Great Commission. We are not to parachute in, throw some money or resources at people, and then bolt before we get dirty. We are to echo Jesus' pattern. Our lives are to be incarnational. By that, I mean we are to do exactly what Jesus did and get our hands dirty. We are to develop relationships with people. We are to support their desire to grow closer to God and lift themselves out of poverty, and we are to be in it for the long haul.

Glimpses of the Coal Mine in Scripture

The value of incarnational ministry is seen all over the New Testament, but begins long before Jesus was born that very first Christmas. The Bible begins with people who live in tents and constantly move around to keep their herds of sheep close to good feeding grounds. When God reveals himself to the people through the law he gives them, he includes in the law instructions for building a tent in which his presence will reside. The tent is called the "tabernacle" and is the meeting place between God and man. It is the very first example of God dwelling among his people.

Later, the book of John describes Jesus in these same terms in 1:14. The typical translation is something like, "The Word became flesh and made his dwelling among us . . ." However, the word translated as "made his dwelling" in the original language is talking about pitching a tent. Jesus was the ultimate fulfillment of what God began in the Judean desert with the tabernacle thousands of years earlier. Jesus was God dwelling with us in the flesh, experiencing all that it means to be human and ultimately suffering to mend the brokenness that we created.

Jesus had an interesting way of doing ministry while he was "in the flesh." Rather than going from synagogue to synagogue giving lectures on the intricacies of the Torah,

Jesus spoke about sheep and home-building. When faced with how to talk about people's receptivity to the Word of God in their life, Jesus decided against a thesis-antithesis-synthesis structure in favor of telling a story about a man sowing seeds along a path. This points to another pattern of Jesus' ministry: contextualization. Jesus was acutely aware of his context, and made sure what he was saying and how he was ministering was relevant and under-standable to those living in that context.

We can see this value of contextualization in the life of Paul and his mission to the Gentiles. He was taking what was a sect of Judaism and transforming it to be something bigger than Judaism as it was understood at that time. He was taking the life and teachings of Jesus and contextualizing them for people who had never cele-brated Passover or made a pilgrimage to Jerusalem. He put it best in 1 Corinthians when he explains his profound commitment to contextualization:

> To the Jews I became like a Jew, to win the Jews. To those under the law I became like one under the law (though I myself am not under the law), so as to win those under the law. To those not having the law I became like one not having the law (though I am not free from God's law but am under Christ's law), so as to win those not having the law. To the weak I became weak, to win the weak. I have become all things to all people so that by all possible means I might save some. (9:20–22)

Though incarnation and contextualization are both incredible in their own right, it is the next missional value that most confounds me: indigenization. Jesus spends about three years getting a good head of steam, is crucified and rises from the dead, and then gathers the disciples on a hill and places the whole thing in their hands. He entrusts the entire enterprise to the judgment of a bunch of fishermen and tax collectors. Before he leaves, he gives them a simple set of instructions, "Therefore go and make disciples of all nations, baptizing them in the name of the Father and of the Son and of the Holy Spirit, and teaching them to obey everything I have commanded you. And surely I am with you always, to the very end of the age" (Matt. 28:19–20).

It's all in their hands. Would they do it the same way Jesus would have done were he running the thing? No. Were they going to make mistakes? Certainly. But Jesus set a huge example of handing ministry over to local people and releasing them to do ministry the way they feel would be best in their context. Wow.

Coal-Mine Moment

"They're running the show down there, not us." My pastor was trying to explain to me the logic of our most recent mission project. We had partnered with a church in a large city in another hemisphere for a couple of years and they had let us know that they were ready to start their first non-church facility project.

When I heard that, I was expecting maybe a maternity clinic or a shelter for street children, or anything other than what I was going to be spending a week working on with fifteen teenagers: a police station. I was a little full of myself and a bit put off at the idea of building a building that would be owned by the city. Everyone in our church knew of all the desperate needs that were there and I am quite confident that none of them, had they been calling the shots, would have chosen this project. It just didn't have the feel-good quality of an orphanage. Instead of pictures of American teens holding third-world babies, we would be in front of a block building with bars on the windows and a city crest on the side.

However, we were committed to letting the locals run the show trusting that, despite our American confidence that they were wrong, the local people knew their needs better than we did. So, we went on the trip, and I was ready to probe the pastor to find out what runaway committee had made this odd decision.

As it turned out, there was no committee. There was unanimous support. "Jeremy, it doesn't matter if people can have a place to send street children if they are afraid to come out of their homes," the pastor explained. "It doesn't matter if they have access to cheap food if it will get stolen from their kitchens before they can eat it."

He was right. Safety is of foundational importance to a community. And, the way that city worked, in order to get different sorts of government help, you had to have a police station. In order to have a police station, the community had to build it themselves and buy a police motorcycle. Armed with understanding and friendships, we came home and raised the money for the needed motorcycle so that when the building was ready, the community had everything in place.

Coal-Mine Ministry

Though these ideals can be applied to ministry as a whole, they are most useful when thinking about these sorts of situations in mission work. Too often, we select mission projects or ministries based on convenience or what we get out of them rather than our theology and beliefs about how ministry should be practiced.

Incarnation is the aspect that can be most difficult for us to value because it requires a commitment to relationship and openness to being vulnerable. It is easy to find options that don't allow for us to be "in the flesh" with the people we are serving. A simple Google search can turn up hundreds of opportunities for you to have a lock-in for the hungry or stay up all night bowling for the needy. While raising money for organizations is helpful, it is not the level of transformation we should look for from mission ministries.

Incarnational mission work means going to the coal mine, getting to know the people, and being the presence of Jesus in their world. Then going back, and talking to the same people and meeting their friends and being a presence of grace in their world. Maybe it is over a bowl of soup or with a warm blanket in the winter, but the goal is the relationship as much as it is the relief. When we miss that, and think that the main goal is to give out toothbrushes or deodorant or sandwiches, we miss the whole Jesus-coming-down-in-the-flesh part of mission work.

When we turn to start thinking about contextualization, we have to think critically about our own culture, which can be quite difficult. Somewhere along the way most of us begin lumping bits of our culture in with our faith as if those pieces of our culture were part of the teachings of Jesus. In the case of Operation Christmas Tree, the piece of our culture that we had made part of our faith was the idea that to properly celebrate Christmas, you had to have a bunch of gifts to unwrap.

Contextualization means looking at what we are doing from the perspective of the culture into which we are coming as partners in mission. Are you taking Vacation Bible School coloring sheets full of English into a primarily Spanish-speaking neighborhood? Are you all wearing crosses on your shirt in a place where wearing a cross is seen as idolatry? Are you assuming control over the work you are doing because they defer to you though they have more experience than you do? The important thing is to constantly ask yourself the question, "Is this coming from my culture or this context?"

Seeking to live out the value of indigenization means two things: letting go of your firmly held conviction that your way is usually right, and believing that there are people in every population you may be serving that have a clearer insight into their own problems and the effectiveness of solutions than you do.

A missionary friend of mine named Sarah Corson told me a story of a ministry she and her husband began in Bolivia. They went down as ministers to this community with a grant of land from the government to build a home/facility to do ministry. When they arrived at the plot, they were overwhelmed by several-foot-high grass that was covering the lot. They hired one of the locals to help maintain the grounds and he set to work cutting the grass, which in that climate turned into a full-time job. After a good tenure, Sarah and her husband left the ministry in the hands of a local man they had trained to take their place, letting the man know they would continue to support the ministry and visit once a year to see how things were going.

When they returned the next year, they got to the plot and were quite upset to see that the new leader had stopped taking care of it. The grass was so high that you couldn't even see the buildings! They confronted him, asking why he had lapsed in his care for the grounds, and he replied that no one cuts grass there. He had taken the man they had been paying to continuously cut grass and continued paying him, but to start a fishery program. Now they had grass like everyone else and a fishery program that was going incredibly well. They were blown away at how blinded they had been by their culture, and were even more committed to the idea of indigenized ministry.

The reality is that most communities know what is needed, and have people with the leadership potential living right there who could spearhead those changes given the right training and support. Our goal is not to send Americans to the foreign land where we met homeless children to start and run an orphanage for the rest of their life. Though it will help the children, it will never be done as effectively as if we go down with the goal of opening an orphanage, training a director, and ensuring lasting support.

Had Operation Christmas Tree been run by someone who had lived in that area or situation, they would have known that arriving at the door carrying gifts humiliates fathers and families. Maybe having a place where they could pick up the presents or setting up a free store where families can come and shop for gifts without having to pay would end up being the appropriate expression of that ministry, but it would be someone from that community who would know best.

The reality is that you may not have the time or luxury to initiate and plan every aspect of your mission programs, but armed with this information, you have a lens through which you can evaluate the potential ministries you will be supporting. Not only that, when someone suggests supporting a ministry that does not share these values, you have a way to explain why you are choosing to support something else.

Coal-Mine Ministers

My career has been full of the opposite of what Wesley did when he moved closer to the coal miners and set up camp to begin ministering there. I have more often than not parachuted in, done something nice, and left as soon as it was over. If I'm honest, more of my non-mission ministry than I'd like to admit is the same way. It is a lot easier to do ministry when you don't get involved in the messy lives of the people you are serving, but that is not the way ahead. We are called to more. We are called to get involved in the lives of the people we are serving, help bear their burdens, and celebrate their victories.

Not only that, we are called to understand their world and its values. You don't have to go halfway around the world to find a different culture. Often walking through the doors of your local high school is enough. And you can tell when people walk through those doors and try and do ministry that is geared for middle-class white adults . . . it doesn't last. Sure, there may be something that catches on for a while, but let the adult leave, and it fizzles out almost immediately. Before we can do ministry, we need to understand the context in which we will be doing ministry. What are the values, the rules, the taboos, the meaning of slang, and the primary method for communication?

Indigenization is pretty clear-cut when talking about partnering in mission with people in your city or in another country, but can be difficult to navigate as a pastor to teens. The reason is that though they are natives, they have generally not developed to the point that they have the self-control, wisdom, and insight to evaluate ministry and envision the path between where they are and the goal ahead. In fact, they may not have developed enough cognitively to make sense of the whole process at all.

That means that turning everything over to be decided upon and run by teens is generally a bad idea and usually ends up with one clique gaining control and all those on the outside of that group fading into the background (and out of the back door) over time. However, this is a commitment to the idea that people who live in a different culture understand that culture better than you do. That means trusting your students' input on whether or not something is "cool" or will be fun. If you give them the role of advisor (rather than decision-maker) they can be an incredible asset to you. Not only that, living out this commitment to indigenization shows your students that you respect their input and realize your own shortcomings.

➡ Personal Processing

1. Of the values discussed in this chapter, which one is most difficult for you to live out? Which one do you find yourself forgetting about?

2. How do these values shape the way that you interact with teens? How does it change your conversations and hang-out time?

3. How does this change how you interact with parents? Take each one and consider how it applies to a conversation with a parent.

4. These often expose areas where we are lacking in humility. What are those areas for you? What is the next step you need to take to be more humble?

➜ Ministry/Team Processing

1. Take a moment to list any ministry or event that you would consider mission-focused.

2. Take time to evaluate each of those ministries. Do they fully support/live out the values of incarnation, contextualization, and indigenization?

3. For those that do not fully support/live out those values, what things could you change about them to align them with this understanding of mission work?

4. What are some ways that these concepts can impact your ministry outside of the realm of mission work?

5. Take a moment to discuss with your team how the personal processing challenged you. What is one thing you want to change or do differently as a result?

9

Bake Sales that Change the World

(Teen Abolitionist Tendencies)

John was nervous. He was so nervous that I told him I'd hang around after class for moral support. Though he had talked to our teacher a thousand times, he was fidgeting as he waited to ask her to buy something, partially because he knew the stuff he was selling was no good and partially because he didn't want to do it. "Mrs. Bea, I'm doing a fund-raiser for my youth group. Would you be interested in buying any of these items?" John handed her the brochure and watched as she perused all the cheaply made trinkets and oddly colored wrapping paper.

"What are you fund-raising for?" she asked.

"My youth group at church," John replied.

"I know, but are you going on a mission trip somewhere or something?"

"No, we are going on a ski trip. I'm so excited. I've never really even seen snow!"

"A ski trip? So, you want me to help you pay for a vacation?"

He was losing her, I could tell, but John was good at selling. He pressed into his pitch: "Kind of. I just want to work for this myself. I didn't want to make my parents pay for it. It's kind of expensive." That was mostly true. He didn't want to ask his parents to pay for it because he knew they wouldn't. They couldn't. If he wanted to go, there was going to be a lot of fund-raising in his future.

Mrs. Bea let him down softly, "I don't really need any of this, John, but here's five dollars to help you on your way."

Five dollars. On our way down the hall John complained that she might as well not have given him anything. But that put his math brain in gear, and as he calculated the percentages in the flyer he realized that most of the items would net him less than Mrs. Bea just donated. Seeing the size of his fund-raising needs, John was turning a corner, "I don't know if it's worth all this. I mean, she's right. It's just a vacation. I feel weird asking people to help me with this."

"But if you don't do it, you can't go right? I know my parents wouldn't be able to send me off to ski for a week," I reminded him.

"Yeah. I don't know. I think I'll just stay home. I don't think many people are going to be able to make that much with this stuff anyway. I didn't sell anything today." He tossed the pamphlet in the trash as we walked by. "Have you ever been on a mission trip?"

"Yeah. It was great." I caught myself before telling the story and said, "Wait, do you mean out of the country?"

"Yeah, I did."

"Oh, then, no. But a friend of mine went to Guatemala, and she came back so pumped that she is just getting money for all her presents for everything this year so she can go back. She was telling me that the people she met there didn't even have enough food to feed their family all the time."

I could see John's passion glinting in his eyes when he responded, "I know! I can't believe that there are still people who have to live that way. I really want to go on a trip like that, and I think it would be easier to get people to buy stuff to help me go, too."

"Totally. My mom gave her like twenty bucks for nothing. I think I might try and go sometime."

• • •

Pointless Fund-raising

I am sure John's youth pastor's heart was in a good place when he planned all the car washes and bake sales that were going to be required for kids like John to be able to afford to go on a ski trip. But what was frustrating for John was that all the effort being put into the fund-raising ended up making no real difference in John's life and definitely none in his world. The one question from his teacher helped him figure out what was really bothering him about the whole venture.

It is my experience that American teens today are in much the same place as John. Their whole world is built around entertaining them, protecting them, and giving them anything they can want or imagine. It all comes with very little effort on their part and when faced with being able to play Xbox over spring break or spending hours raising funds to go on a ski (or beach) trip, very few of them choose the work. But why?

Why do they not jump at the chance to go with a bunch of friends to the mountains or the beach? Why is a little bit of work such a deterrent when the final trip would be so awesome? I believe it is because it doesn't capture their hearts. While it would be fun to go to those places and do those things, it is also fun going a couple of hours away to the small place people in their city go for a good time.

More than that, the church has something bigger to offer them: being part of the work of God in the world. During this stage of development, students are searching for their place in the world. They need to discover what they have to offer and how they can make an impact in big problems. This is the moment where they are asking the question, "Can my life really matter?" The answer of the church is, and always has been, yes!

Abolition Ministry

Wesley and the movement his work spawned never shied away from tackling big problems in practical ways. One of the most major moments for the Methodist movement in America centered around ending the oppression that was American slavery. From the very beginning, slavery was an issue within the Methodist church. Indeed, at the very first conference meeting those gathered made it clear that slavery was not biblical or moral. All Methodists were instructed to free their slaves. Over the intervening decades that policy was softened, but there was an abiding commitment to abolition. Eventually it all came to a head with a messy situation involving a slave-holding bishop that resulted in a north/south split of the movement in 1844.

The leaders of the Methodist Church in America, Francis Asbury and Thomas Coke, were passionate about this issue, and gave a significant portion of their lives to pushing against it. At one point they were able to arrange a meeting with George Washington to try to convince him to free his slaves. Though he didn't free his slaves immediately, not long after the meeting, he altered his will to free all of his slaves upon his death.

Their care for the slaves did not stay confined to church and national politics. Their efforts were hands-on and intensely practical as well. The Methodist Church was one of the few churches that reached out to slaves and helped develop worshipping communities for slaves that were led by their peers or former slaves. By 1816, about one-fourth (42,304) of the members of the Methodist Church were black, and of those, three-fourths were in the South.[12] What an amazing history! Though they were fighting even within their own ranks for the freedom of these people, they did not allow their (sometimes horrific) arguments over the status of these brothers and sisters to prevent them from reaching out and caring for their souls.

This is the pattern throughout history with this movement. We are neither afraid to make a stand for grace and peace nor to disregard the raging debate and continue to minister despite the contention within our ranks. We are a people who get our hands dirty in the things that matter in our world and never cease proclaiming the love and grace of God to everyone everywhere.

Glimpses of Abolition in Scripture

This pattern of getting involved in the issues of the time can be seen throughout Scripture, and when looking for examples you need to look no further than the life of

Jesus. In Jesus' day there was a big debate over where and how you were to worship. The division was between two groups who claimed to be worshipping the same God. One of them worshipped in Jerusalem, while the other worshipped on a mountain on the other side of the tracks. The debate was so heated that they weren't even supposed to talk to each other.

What did Jesus do? He crossed to the other side of the tracks and struck up a conversation with a woman with a less-than-stellar reputation: "'Woman,' Jesus replied, 'believe me, a time is coming when you will worship the Father neither on this mountain nor in Jerusalem. . . . Yet a time is coming and has now come when the true worshipers will worship the Father in the Spirit and in truth, for they are the kind of worshipers the Father seeks'" (John 4:21, 23). Jesus went beyond addressing the current theological debate, using the opportunity to free her from sin and offer her the gift of forgiveness.

Another group of outcasts in Jesus' day were those that dealt with various skin conditions all lumped together under the term "leprosy" in the Bible. These people were such outcasts that they were not to be touched. Jesus does not let their contagious skin conditions stop him from ministering to them. Instead, when he is presented with the opportunity to minster to these outcasts, he touches them and heals them

It doesn't stop with Jesus; Paul also breaks down barriers and ministers despite opposition. Before Paul comes along, Christianity is just a sect within Judaism. Then, out of nowhere, Paul gets a mission direct from God to mess up the whole Jew/Gentile dichotomy. Paul, knowing the divide between Jew and Gentile, believes that God is calling him to minister to these non-covenant participants. Even though he knows it will cause an uproar, even though he knows he may get censured, he sets off to minister to the outsiders.

Over and over in the Bible, we are given examples of people taking stands and ministering to those who are not on the inside while critiquing the peculiar theology that had been excluding so many from God's plan for the world. This is who we are in the Scriptures and history. It is who God desires us to be in life, and it is a unique opportunity to reach those who are looking to be part of something bigger than themselves.

Abolitionist Moment

Our smallest attendance month for a long time was August. Between the last-ditch vacations and doing everything required to start school, it was a ghost town. We were sitting in the volunteer decompression chamber at a summer camp lamenting the upcoming trough before we hit our stride in fall. "I feel like we are giving up by not planning anything compelling in August." I continued, "I know no one comes then, but how much of the lull is because we totally give up the month and just get ready for fall?"

Though it was only a glimmer of hope in our history-based skepticism, we held onto it and began to dream. "What if we did something completely different? What if we tried to equip students to make a difference in their world? What would that look like?" That was the tipping point. Our hopes and dreams for equipping students to do ministry broke out and began to create a chain reaction of how we might see the kingdom of God break forth at the hands of our students. That night at camp we told the students that this August was going to be different. It was going to be about doing something about their faith. No details now . . . just get ready. We repeated this announcement over the next several weeks as we finished our planning.

All too quickly, the first week of August was upon us and we had no idea if there would be anyone there. To our astonishment, we had more students there than we had in attendance in the spring before, and the second week was bigger than the first. The most amazing part for us was that on the last Sunday of August we had fifteen small student-designed and student-led ministries launch to work on everything from modern-day slavery to homelessness in our city.

Abolitionist Ministry

What all of this says to us is that our ministries need to be offering people a way to engage in the meaningful debates and global issues of their time. They need to not only be given insight into what kinds of things are happening in the world, but offered a means by which they can be part of the solution.

This can, of course, be difficult with teenagers because they may not have the resources or authority to make significant strides in bringing a real solution to problems like global hunger or the increasing urban slum population across the world. However, just because they cannot start a multinational nonprofit to end world hunger does not mean that they cannot contribute meaningfully to the solution. There are two things that teens can do to impact almost any problem.

The first of those paths for action is raising awareness. Not many people know that one in eight people on the planet live in an urban slum. Even less realize what that actually means. Students in one group did research online about urban slums in a specific country, then constructed a slum village in the grass next to the church parking lot and all day and night living in the slums. They erected a banner that read, "1.8 Billion People Live in Urban Slums" that everyone could see when they drove in to church that Sunday.

That would have raised a lot of awareness, but the students took it a step further. They developed a tour of their slum village, describing the plight of urban slum dwellers and offering people a look into the daily life of 1.8 billion people. During the announcements at church that morning everyone was encouraged to take a tour of the slums after the service was over, and hundreds of people got to know more about this pressing global issue that had no clue before they showed up that morning.

The second path for action is raising funds to support the organizations that are making a difference in a problem that is difficult for people to directly impact. A perfect example of this is the global slave and sex trafficking industry. There are more people enslaved today than at the height of the transatlantic slave trade. That problem is very difficult to impact, especially when you are a twelve-year-old girl in Alabama. However, you can raise funds for organizations like the International Justice Mission that employs international lawyers and former FBI agents to help foreign governments raid, convict, and crack down on people engaging in this horrible practice.

What if, instead of doing all your car washes and bake sales to send a couple of kids to camp for free, you did a bake sale to free slaves or a car wash to stop malaria? What if your garage sale provided clean birthing kits for mothers who were delivering babies in the slums or was sending kids to school in a village in South America? All of a sudden, the laborious, tedious work is transformed. Now it is imbued with rich meaning and significance. It is not just another act to benefit oneself, but a vehicle for making a difference in a huge problem. It is a way to engage in an issue that matters.

Abolitionist Ministers

As a pastor, getting people to go to your ministries and events can become an overriding concern, especially when you know that they might not be able to afford it. You don't want money to be the issue so you start organizing fund-raiser after fund-raiser to help them pay their way. All of a sudden, your ministry seems to be more about fund-raising than Jesus.

When this becomes the pattern, it teaches students that their faith really is all about them and that the concerns in their world are secondary. It says to those that are passionate about a cause, "Wait, we have to pay for our trips first. We'll get to your idea after we have done something for ourselves."

What our history of being engaged with big issues and ministering to those involved tells us is that a huge part of our role as pastors is channeling the passion of people to make a difference into the cause of Christ in the world. It means taking the words in the Lord's Prayer seriously: "Thy kingdom come, thy will be done on earth as it is in heaven." It means coming to the realization that sometimes the best thing you can do is cancel your ski trip and spend all that money on feeding the homeless in your community.

In order to do that it means that we have to stay informed on global issues. It means that we need to be considering what Jesus would have us do about these problems and finding organizations that are worthy of our support. Finally, it means teaching and modeling a faith that demands action against injustice and releasing people to act upon their faith.

➡ Personal Processing

1. How much time have you spent thinking about these kinds of issues?

2. How good are you at helping people find their passion and harness it for the kingdom?

3. What issue captures your heart? What can you do to make a difference in it?

→ **Ministry/Team Processing**

1. Think about your ministries. Where are students most likely to be given the opportunity to advocate for the victims of injustice?

2. When is there a time in the next month or two that you could spend several weeks teaching on injustice and helping students find both the issues that capture their heart and a way to make a difference in those issues?

3. How can what you are doing branch out of your area of responsibility? How can it be an example of what it means to be a Christian in your broader community?

4. How much of your fund-raising efforts in the past year have gone for something other than a trip or event you were putting on for your church? How can you increase that percentage?

5. Take a moment to discuss with your team how the personal processing challenged you. What is one thing you want to change or do differently as a result?

EPILOGUE

We just don't do that." I was in a planning meeting for an event where we had a new volunteer pushing for a very non-Wesleyan idea.

"Why?" The volunteer was surprised that I didn't jump on the idea.

As I looked around the room of staff and volunteers, I asked, "Do any of you know why?" They didn't, and my heart sank. My heart sank because what bubbled out was practical responses of "It's not cool" or "Kids just don't like that kind of stuff anymore." The "why" was much bigger. The volunteer's idea was clearly in opposition to the prevenient grace that was the focus of this specific event. I knew I had to do something about this.

All of the responses my staff and volunteers gave were okay, but I wanted our "what" to be fueled by how we see God. I want our whole ministry to be painting the picture of God the way we understand him. I want everyone on my team to know that how we do ministry comes from what we believe about God.

That's when we went through the content in this book. Over several weeks we talked about prevenient grace, coal mines, and abolition. We dreamed about how these deep beliefs could transform our ministry and began to work on how that might happen.

To call what happened an "awakening" might be too strong, but for me it seems about right. In my planning meetings and casual conversations I began to hear people talk about God, grace, and how that impacts our practice of ministry. I watched as this theological understanding of ministry spread throughout our group until people not only could answer in theological terms why we would or wouldn't do something, but would walk up and say things like, "I just had a great idea for how we could explore justifying grace!" Win.

I know every ministry book you've read has said something like this, and to be honest my publisher is going to love the next sentence. Your whole team needs to read this book. I say this because I have seen the results and can tell you that if you care enough about theology informing practice to have read this far, the next step is simple. Assemble the team, and journey together through this material. You won't regret it!

NOTES

1. Outler, Albert C. (2010-09-01). *John Wesley's Sermons: An Anthology* (Kindle Locations 10401–10402). Abingdon Press. Kindle Edition.

2. Albert C. Outler, *John Wesley's Sermons* (Nashville, TN: Abingdon Press, 1991), 1:381.

3. John Wesley, *Works,* Vol. 10 (New York: Harper, 1827), 148.

4. For those who are not familiar with "the hive of scum and villainy" reference, please put this book down and watch the original *Star Wars* movie immediately.

5. John Wesley and Charles Wesley, "The Nature, Design, and General Rules of the United Societies, in London, Bristol, Kingswood, Newcastle-upon-Tyne" in *The Works of John Wesley*, Vol. 8, 3rd ed. (London: Wesleyan Methodist Book Room, 1872), 270–71.

6. Richard P. Heitzenrater, *Wesley and the People Called Methodists,* 2nd ed. (Nashville, TN: Abingdon Press, 1995, 2013), Kindle edition, 3136–37.

7. Kenneth J. Collins, *The Theology of John Wesley: Holy Love and the Shape of Grace* (Nashville, TN: Abingdon Press, 2007), Kindle edition, 251.

8. John Wesley, "Rules of the band societies, drawn up December 25, 1738" available online: https://archive .org/stream/rulesofbandsocie468wesl#page/4/mode/2up.

9. "Theological Guidelines" available online: http:// archives.umc.org/interior.asp?mid=1664.

10. Heitzenrater, *Wesley and the People Called Methodists*, 1809.

11. John Wesley, "December 6, 1739" available online: http://wesley.nnu.edu/john-wesley/the-letters-of-john -wesley/wesleys-letters-1739/.

12. Minutes from the 1816 Annual Conference. Available online: http://books.google.com/books?id=vj4m AQAAIAAJ&lpg=PA265&ots=xnMnhL8nOl&dq=1816% 20methodist%20conference%20minutes&pg=PA282#v =onepage&q=negro&f=false.